Your *Dream* RECORD BOOK

D1317106

Your
Dream
RECORD BOOK

A Diary and Guide to Interpreting Your Dreams

CHARTWELL
BOOKS, INC.

This edition printed in 2006 by

CHARTWELL BOOKS, INC.
A Division of **BOOK SALES, INC.**
114 Northfield Avenue
Edison, New Jersey 08837

Copyright © 2006 Arcturus Publishing Limited
26/27 Bickels Yard, 151–153 Bermondsey Street,
London SE1 3HA

All rights reserved. No part of this publication may be reproduced,
stored in a retrieval system, or transmitted, in any form or by any
means, electronic, mechanical, photocopying, recording or otherwise,
without written permission in accordance with the provisions of the
Copyright Act 1956 (as amended). Any person or persons who do any
unauthorised act in relation to this publication may be liable to
criminal prosecution and civil claims for damages.

ISBN-13: 978-0-7858-2165-6
ISBN-10: 0-7858-2165-1

Printed in China

Introduction

The human desire to explore and interpret dreams dates back thousands of years and is universal to cultures and civilizations all over the world. Ancient peoples set great store by seeing dreams as prophetic visions that were sent by deities to guide human behaviour in a world where natural phenomena such as volcanoes and earthquakes were regarded as warnings and punishments sent from the heavens.

Evidence of the old beliefs in dreams can be found in the Bible and in the writings of the fourth-century Greek prophet Artemidorus, and many of the dream interpretations of ancient times remained largely unchanged until the development of psychoanalytic theory in the nineteenth century. With the work of Freud, Jung and others came an understanding of the subconscious and the way that our minds, during the process of dreaming, reorder the thoughts and experiences we have with our logical brains while we are awake. Some therapists of the time held that dreams could not be interpreted without their professional help, and there was a tendency to be prescriptive about what they meant. As theories advanced, however, it became understood that much depended upon the personality of the dreamer, and that dreamers themselves could interpret what relevance their dreams had to their own psychologies and realities.

To begin to interpret your own dreams you will need to keep a dream diary, recording not only those which seem significant but also more minor ones. As your interpretive skills develop you may begin to see patterns emerge that were not evident from apparently random dreams of little consequence. If you awake from a dream that seems particularly important you may wish to carry a notebook with you that day in case anything of relevance to the dream occurs to you.

Dreams are quickly forgotten, and you will need to record them as soon as you wake. This can be done by having a recording device of some type on your bedroom table, or simply a pen and a notepad. To help you access your presence in the dream later, record it in the present tense rather than the past. Note the main elements or feelings first, followed by the more minor details. If you wish to explore your dreams in great detail, creating a computer database with which you can examine the recurrences of symbols or beings will help. Include notes of how and with whom you spent the day before each dream.

Then, when you are ready to interpret a dream, examine the meaning of each of the main elements and try to find an overall theme. Exploring your dreams with friends or relatives who know you well and are able to provide an objective interpretation can be immensely helpful in giving you new insights.

Once you have begun to interpret your dreams you will find you will wish to explore this fascinating manifestation of the workings of the human mind using theories and techniques gained from many sources. This book will act as a valuable stepping stone on a path towards your greater understanding of your waking mind and the world in which you live.

Interpreting
your dreams

In this section of the book you will find a list of
many of the most common elements that occur in
dreams, along with some more unusual ones too.
The interpretations given come from ancient
sources as well as from Romany lore and
psychoanalytic thought.

Abandonment

that dreadful feeling that someone you trusted has left you totally on your own, drifting around in an unknown landscape, is often a reflection that when you were a child, you were constantly afraid that you were unwanted by others in the family. Ninety-nine times out of a hundred this is completely untrue, but the fear lingers on into adulthood and surfaces in the dreamer's mind as abandonment. When it appears regularly, the dreamer is often the type of person who has difficulty laying down plans to safeguard the future. It can mean trouble ahead, but if the dreamer takes it as a warning, then the trouble can usually be averted.

Abdomens

suggest that the dreamer has put himself in a vulnerable position, probably in a recent business venture or in a shift in responsibilities in the workplace. To dream of a large abdomen is indicative of the dreamer's hopes of good times ahead, while to see a small stomach is indicative that the dreamer fears that the road ahead is not going to be particularly smooth.

Abdominal pains

are said, in converse manner, to tell dreamers not just that they are in a reasonably good state of health but that their lungs are strong and their legs especially shapely! But if the pains are in the lower abdomen then the horizon could become clouded by family problems.

Abduction

this may not be one of the most common of dreams, but when it does snatch the dreamer's attention, it is likely that he has been facing some sort of opposition, maybe in business or perhaps socially. The dream is a sign that this will be overcome and the desired success is waiting to be embraced. And if the dreamer witnesses someone being abducted, then some unexpected good news is imminent.

Abhorrence

when it is the dominant emotion in a dream, this is a warning that danger and difficult times lie ahead. Usually they will present themselves from out of the blue and their influence on the dreamer's life depends on the degree of the emotion that is aroused. If it is intensely felt, then the potential to do harm is great, but if it is more strong annoyance than true abhorrence, then the difficulties will be easily overcome. Romanies believed that when the dreamer experienced abhorring someone, they would often be strongly suspicious of a person's behaviour and that these suspicions would prove to be well founded. If, on the other hand, it is the dreamer who sees himself as being held in abhorrence, then currently held good intentions to act for the general benefit in some scheme or other will slowly fade away to be replaced by selfish motives coming to the fore. And if the dreamer is a young woman whose affections are unengaged and she sees herself being abhorred by a lover, then she will fall in love. Sadly, the man with whom she eventually gives her heart may prove to be someone she will come to dislike intensely but from whom she will be unable to part.

Abroad

whether it be in a country the dreamer recognizes or an unfamiliar one, is an indication of a deeply felt need for personal freedom. Being abroad in a dream may indicate a desire to escape from a physical location or perhaps from a relationship or situation. To gypsies, it had two very straightforward meanings. Either that the dreamer was about to go travelling (very likely if the dreamer was also a gypsy) in the company of good friends,

9

or that it may be necessary to leave one's present whereabouts and go and live abroad – again quite likely given the gypsies' well-known dislike of being in one place for any great length of time. Another interpretation is that if the dreamer sees him or herself as travelling abroad by sea, then he or she may be about to make friends with people of considerable influence in the near future.

Absconding

the meaning of absconding in the dream almanac depends on the sex of the dreamer. For men to either see themselves absconding or others doing so is an indication that colleagues at work may have smiles on their faces when they look at the dreamer, but scowls and sneers when he is out of view! And to women, a similar dream should be taken as a warning to be extremely careful when deciding on whom to bestow affection.

Absence

either someone not being where they should be, or the absence of something that could be reasonably expected to be where it is not, can be taken as an indication that the unexpected is about to strike. And as it's unexpected, the dreamer is given no indication of when or where it will come from, or what form it will take! On a deep psychological level, a dream of absence can be a spillover from the emotions felt when the child noticed for the first time that a parent (usually the mother) was not there. On a less serious note, if you dream that you are happy about the absence of a friend, then an enemy could be about to leave the scene. Whereas to dream of a sense of deep loss at the absence of someone suggests that at some time in the past the dreamer acted hastily and unwisely in doing something that is now deeply regretted. And in repenting for the deed, the foundations of a life-lasting friendship will be laid.

Abundance

means the opposite in dreams of what it means in life – for if you dream that there is a great abundance of something it is a clear warning to conserve resources for they could be about to be drained. A more traditional interpretation was that if a dreamer saw himself abundantly provided for Fortune would not so much smile on the dreamer's material life, she would positively grin. But it is a different matter on the domestic front; as riches come in the door, happiness slips out the window as his or her partner seeks comfort in someone else's arms.

Abuse

the meaning of abuse depends on whether the dreamer is the abuser or the abused. If the former, then if you have acted in any way dishonourably towards friends, repercussions will be felt. Such antisocial behaviour can also mean that financial losses are on the cards because of an obstinate refusal to see that good money is being thrown after bad. If the dreamer is being abused, physically, verbally or emotionally, there is a strong likelihood that enemies will gain the upper hand, unless the dreamer takes what he sees as a warning to be on guard.

Abusive language

when heard in a woman's dream suggests that she will become the focus of another's jealousy and envy. If it is she who is doing the swearing, society is about to turn its collective back on her because the unkindness she displayed towards friends in the past is about to become public knowledge.

An abyss

is a reflection of the dreamer's recognition that at some time in life we all must come face to face with the unknown, which, when we face it, will cause us to take risks we have never even contemplated before. It can also suggest the dreamer's fear of losing control, or of a loss of identity or being seen as a failure. This may act as the spur to lead him or her on to exceed the self-imposed boundaries and become a stronger, more complete person. If there is a danger of falling into the abyss then a problem that is being currently faced will be seen off. But to stagger and fall into it is to warn the dreamer that if he or she is to avoid a business loss he or she will have to be extremely careful. Romany folk believed that a dream in which an abyss features is a warning that someone has their eyes on your property and may be willing to resort to law to get their hands on it. Such a chasm may also portend that personal life in the immediate future will be marked by arguments that will be particularly vicious.

Accidents

happen to all of us and feature widely in dreams. Such dreams serve as a warning to steer clear of whatever was involved in the dream accident no matter what. Many dreamers claim that heeding such warnings has saved their lives. For example, one dreamer who saw himself being in a car accident took to taking the bus to work. A few days later he passed an extremely bad crash at the exact spot he would have been and at the exact time he would have been there had he driven to work. If the dreamer sees himself as being badly injured, he should take it as a warning to beware the hidden aggression of others. Accidents can also highlight anxieties about safety and fears about taking on responsibilities. If the accident happens to an animal, then according to gypsy tradition, the dreamer will have to struggle with all his might to achieve what it is he wants and in attaining it, a friend or colleague will suffer a corresponding loss. If a public convenience is the cause of the accident, then the dreamer may well be about to suffer a loss or is in danger of being struck down by illness. If the dreamer is a young woman and she sees herself involved in a particularly bad accident, then her lover may well be planning to desert her without warning.

Acid

signifies an awareness that there is something corrosive in the dreamer's life, which may be the cause of some unhappiness but which could be turned to the dreamer's advantage. It can also suggest that the dreamer feels that his self confidence is being eroded by circumstances beyond his control. The first step to getting it back is to recognize what is happening. A woman seeing herself drinking acid in her dreams denotes that she is about to be compromised and that as a result her health may be endangered. And for dreamers of either sex to see bottles of acid neatly stacked on a shelf is a warning that the stench of treachery is in the air.

Adolescents

if of the opposite sex, suggest that the dreamer is suppressing a part of his or her development. If the dreamer sees himself as he was as an adolescent then he may be acknowledging that some part of himself has still to mature. Often dreams of adolescence say that the dreamer wants more freedom to act as he wants and that he or she resents the freedom which others seem to enjoy.

Adultery

an increasingly common fact of modern life if divorce statistics are a reliable indicator of sexual as well as social mores, suggests that the dreamer is trying, or realizes he ought to try, to come to terms with his sexual needs and desires for stimulation and excitement. Dreaming of having an affair is the dreamer's way of releasing these feelings. Affairs may also be the psyche's way of seeking emotional satisfaction in our dreams in ways that are taboo when we are awake. If the dreamer sees his or her spouse as having an affair, this could be an expression of feelings of sexual inadequacy. Dream interpreters of days gone by held that the dreamer who saw himself committing adultery was prescient that some previously unknown criminal misdemeanour was about to be revealed and that the long arm of the law was about to tap the dreamer on the shoulder. If the dreamer was a female, her dream adultery was a warning to control her temper lest her spiteful outbursts drive her husband to another's arms. And if she recognized her illicit dream lover as being a friend of her husband's her husband would, for no reason she could ascertain, pay less and less attention to her. Finally, if she saw herself as attempting to entice a much younger man into her bed, her husband might be about to leave her and initiate divorce proceedings.

Advice

given and advice received have their own meanings. To receive it in a dream tells us that we should listen to our 'inner voices' more than we do and that we should act on our instincts more than we do at present. It can also be an indication that we have been asked to do something and have agreed to it, despite the fact that we don't really want to. To dream of giving advice displays a willingness to share what we have – be it physical, spiritual or emotional – with others.

Affairs

suggest that the dreamer needs to come to terms with his or her sexual needs and desires if he or she is to be a really rounded person. Seeing himself or herself enjoying illicit company is also a sign that it is not just sex that should be attended to. Perhaps the dreamer is aware that other aspects of his or her life are out of balance and need attention.

Afternoons

may not feature often in dreams, but if they are what a female remembers as being the dominant theme, she can look forward to new friendships – not superficial, social acquaintances, but deep friendships that will be enjoyed for the rest of her life.

AIDS

as a late twentieth-century fact of life is a very recent addition to the dream journal, and is seen as an expression of a deep-rooted fear of being permanently scarred in life. This may not be concerned with health – it could be that a bad career choice has ruined life. To dream that someone else has AIDS is indicative of a feeling of helplessness regarding some situation in which the dreamer is involved.

Alabaster

is a sign of success in marriage and in any legal disputes. But if the dream ends with a piece of figure cast from this cool, elegant stone dropped and broken, then sorrow looms and the dreamer will be called upon to repent of something done in the distant past. If the dreamer is a young woman and she sees herself opening an alabaster box then some careless action will result in the loss of something she holds dear – property perhaps, or her lover.

Aliens

signify that something frightening but unknown may have to be faced in the near future. But they can also suggest that the dreamer is aware that he or she is different in some way from

15

others and is slowly realizing that this is nothing to worry about: we are all different in our own ways and life is richer for it. On the other hand, to dream that you are an alien could be a warning that an interest in the occult is taking too strong a hold. If the dream concerns being abducted by aliens, this may be an expression of a fear of change, especially in domestic affairs. Gypsies believed that when aliens appeared in dreams, their presence meant that the dreamer would meet people whom he considered to be peculiar and in whose company the dreamer would, at first, feel uncomfortable. But the more they can get to know each other, the more the dreamer can relax in their company and the more influential they will become.

Alligators

and their cousins, crocodiles, have few natural enemies in the wild, but are the enemies of many creatures who cohabit their territories. Dreams of being attacked by one of these lethal, toothy aquatic creatures suggest that the dreamer is insecure in many aspects of life and is especially concerned that enemies are plotting against him.

Amethyst

is good news for businessmen, bad news for young women who have recently become engaged. To the former it is full order books and excellent sales; to the latter it warns that the engagement may be broken off.

Anger

is a commonly experienced emotion and is often felt in dreams where it is seen as representing the struggle to express ourselves properly. Anger, when it dominates a dream, can also be interpreted as the mind's way of telling the dreamer that it is quite in order for him or her to feel passionately about something – and to give verbal expression to that passion. If the anger is focused on someone the dreamer knows, the obvious interpretation is that that person has offended the dreamer and the dream is an expression of pent-up hostility. This, again, may be the result of being unable to express the anger in real life, for fear of causing offence. If the anger is being directed at the dreamer, then this is most likely a guilt thing: the dreamer is aware that he is responsible for something unsavoury and has not yet said, 'Sorry!' although he knows an apology is due. Traditional folklore held that when anger makes its presence felt, some terrible trial awaits the dreamer. It could concern being let down badly by a loved one, or that the ties that bind a long-valued friendship are about to be cut. It could even be that enemies who have been plotting the dreamer's downfall are about to see their plans come to successful fruition. If the dream concerns friends or family being angry with the dreamer, he or she may be about to be called upon to mediate in some dispute – and will do so successfully. According to one nineteenth-century sage, anger denotes that enemies whose plots will threaten the dreamer's security and happiness surround the dreamer, and that a rival for a lover's hand is whispering slander in his or her ear. A contemporary interpretation suggests that to dream of being angry with one's spouse was a signal that a period of unusual peace and harmony lay ahead on the domestic front. A less fanciful meaning is that anger in a dream is representative of other passionate emotions and that the dreamer is struggling to find the right way to express them.

Antelopes

indicate that if you strive, achieving your highest ambitions is more than likely. Sadly, if a young woman sees an antelope slip, the love she hopes to win will prove her downfall.

17

Apes

swinging through the dream landscape bring humiliation or ill-ness to a dear one. If the ape is clinging to a tree then beware, for you have a false friend who is about to cause ill-feeling in your family or extended family circle.

Appetites

do not commonly feature in dreams, but, according to one sage of days gone by, when someone wakes up and recalls that he or she has appeased the appetite by eating something of which he or she is particularly fond, ill health is about to afflict the dreamer with a noticeable effect on the dreamer's appearance. He goes on to write that to be conscious of being hungry in a dream is a sign that good friends are about to leave the scene, and that a failing appetite heralds bad news. Modern, more sci-entific interpreters suggest that such dreams represent an unful-filled desire either physical or spiritual. Appetite is also thought to be indicative of an especially lusty nature.

Apples

in spite of their notorious history involving the downfall of man and expulsion from the Garden of Eden, apples are generally regarded as fortuitous in dreams. Walking through apple trees can indicate fruitfulness and since medieval times has been seen as suggesting a time of good harvest, which today can mean success in business. If, however, there are many fallen apples and you inadvertently walk upon them, that promise is compromised. One source suggests that if you dream of eating a sweet apple you are due for an unspecified happy event. A sour apple suggests exactly the opposite. To dream of an apple tree means that good news is about to drop through the letter box, but only if the tree is alive and flourishing. If it's dead, then beware the postman's tread, for bad tidings are in his bag.

Applying make-up

denotes success in life. If the dreamer is in love, it indicates that her sweetheart is faithful, good-humoured and keen to tie the knot as quickly as possible. If the dreamer is already married, then any children she has will be very successful. To see someone else putting their make-up on is to be warned that false friends have unpleasant surprises in store.

Appointments

suggest that the dreamer is aware that his or her life is lacking goals and that now is the time to start aiming for success. But if the dreamer misses an appointment, then this is indicative of an awareness that not enough attention is being paid to the details of life. Appointments can also suggest that the dreamer feels that he or she is due a reward for something that has been done and is feeling resentful that such reward has not been forthcoming.

Aprons

can represent family ties or perhaps a badge of office. But their meaning, like so much in the dreamer's dictionary, depends on the dreamer's gender. To an unmarried woman aprons were thought to signify that she would meet and eventually marry a wealthy man, but that for the marriage to be successful she would have to use all her skills and wiles to keep him. To a married woman, the appearance of an apron promised that her children would be a source of immense pride once they had completed their education and embarked on their careers. To male dreamers who see themselves wearing an apron it suggests that a great deal of diplomatic skill is going to be needed to extricate themselves from a potentially embarrassing situation. If someone else is wearing an apron then that person may soon be looking to the dreamer for protection.

Arenas

signify that a decision has been made about the dreamer that will involve a move into a new, specially created environment: perhaps an employer is so impressed that a new position has been created specifically with the dreamer in mind. They can also be an expression of an awareness that a conflict that has been lingering in the background for some time should be brought out into the open and dealt with if it is not to fester like a bad wound and seep into other areas of the dreamer's life.

Arms

wrap themselves around the dreamer in a variety of ways, each of which has its own meaning. For a man to dream that his arms have become bigger and stronger means the male members of his family will help him to achieve his dreams of wealth. The same dream experienced by a woman tells her that her husband will grow in rank and status. Strong arms generally are a good sign. Generally they indicate good fortune. More particularly, if the dreamer is unwell, then he is well on the way to recovery, and if the dreamer is in prison he will soon be free. Broken arms in a male dream signify loss of authority in career matters or that a male relative will suffer ill health. If the dreamer is a woman, the same dream warns that her husband may fall seriously ill and worse, he may not recover. Death of a male relative or friend is also presaged by a dream of an arm having being cut off. If the dreamer sees the arm being amputated then death is also forewarned: a male friend or relative if it is the right arm, female if it is the left.

Assassins

are as unwelcome in dreams as they are in real life, for to dream of being killed by one says that try as you might, whatever you strive for will never be achieved. To see someone else being assassinated, and if there is fresh blood on the body, is a warning that an enemy will play a particularly dirty trick on the dreamer to bring him low. Assassins also warn that unknown enemies may be about to cause the dreamer considerable financial loss. If the dreamer is a woman, the presence of an assassin in her dreams suggests that she is scared that something she had hoped would remain secret for ever may be about to be revealed and that the revelation will cause her considerable embarrassment and distress.

Attics

relate to the past and often indicate that the dreamer feels that he has failed to achieve what was expected of him by his parents when he was younger.

Autopsies

unpleasant as they may be in real life, are welcome when seen in dreams where they point to new and interesting experiences down the road (often of a sexual nature).

Autumn

has little meaning in the male dream landscape, but when it colours the dreams of a woman, she is being told that she will gain some sort of advantage – maybe a financial windfall – not through her own efforts, but through the hard work of others. If she is unmarried and sees herself an autumn bride, then her marriage will be a good one and she will have an especially happy home life.

Avalanches

suggest that while we may feel we are coping with life, deep down we fear that we are being overwhelmed. So, in that context, they are telling the dreamer that he or she should take steps to regain control of outside forces. Another interpretation is that obstacles are about to crash into the dreamer's life and there is absolutely nothing that can be done about them. Oddly, though, if the dreamer sees him or herself being buried in an avalanche, spectacular good fortune may be on its way. If others are being swept away in a landslide then a change in surroundings is indicated.

Babies

tell us that we have to recognize that we have feelings deep inside us over which we have absolutely no control and probably never will have. Very often babies feature in our dreams when we are planning a new venture. If the baby is someone else's rather than one's own the dreamer is being reminded that other people have the ability to hurt and should always be treated with respect. If the baby is a particularly bonny one, new opportunities could be about to present themselves and if grasped, they could be exploited to the dreamer's advantage. If it is crying and obviously not well, then the opportunities could well lead to increased responsibilities. Dreaming of giving a baby away suggests that the dreamer feels overburdened with responsibility and wants to lighten his or her load.

Babies' rattles

to young women, rattles herald an early marriage and that babies will be quick to follow. To others, they say that little will shake the dreamer's contentment, that home life will be happy, and that on the job front, things will go well.

Backache

warns a female dreamer that unless she wraps up when she ventures out, even for a moment, in bad weather, then she will be stricken with illness.

Bags

are generally a good thing to see in your dreams. If you are carrying one that is full, you might not acquire great wealth, but you will never go short. If it is so full that you can hardly carry it, let alone shut it, then significant wealth will be yours. But if the bag is hanging loosely from its strap and is obviously empty, then poverty may well afflict you.

Bailiffs

suggest that the dreamer has serious doubts as to his or her abilities to manage his or her resources and is increasingly aware that he or she may have gone too far in some respect and is fearful of soon being held accountable for doing so. Bailiffs also indicate that we suspect we have not fulfilled our obligations as efficiently as we might have and have put ourselves at risk, which will cause us material loss unless we take responsibility for our actions. To Romany folk, the appearance of bailiffs said that the dreamer was striving to get on in life, but that a lack of intellect would hold him or her back. And if the bailiff marched the dreamer off (or in the case of women, made love to them!) then that was a warning that acquaintances who pretended to be friends were scheming to impoverish the dreamer in some way.

Bait

being laid by a woman to trap or lure a household pest is seen as her having serious doubts in her ability to attract a suitable partner, and because of this she feels that she may have to resort to trickery to find herself happily settled. To dreamers of both sexes, bait can also be an indication that something that has been kept hidden needs to be brought out into the open if their full potential is to be achieved. To do this, some sort of self-help techniques may have to be resorted to. On a spiritual level, the dream may suggest that before anything seen as evil in the dreamer's life can be discarded, it may have to be 'trapped' in some way.

Balance

in the waking world can be taken two ways: it can have either a physical or financial meaning. If we dream that we are trying to maintain our balance, then the interpretation is quite straight-forward – something is out of kilter in our lives and we are struggling to find a way to regain our equilibrium. If the dream concerns balancing our finances then we are acknowledging that we are lacking something in our lives but that we are not sure what that something is. If the dream concerns balance in a mercantile sense – i.e. we have been shortchanged – then the dreamer may be awakening to the fact that he has a good deal more intelligence than he (or the people he knows) has realized.

Baldness

in other people is an acknowledgement that the dreamer is growing ever more aware that his or her life is becoming increasingly dull. It can also suggest that someone may be work-ing against the dreamer in some way, but he won't succeed as long as the dreamer keeps his wits about him. On a deeper level, baldness is a recognition that the dreamer is con-cerned about the spiritual side of life and would like to pay it more attention. And according to folklore, to dream of a bald-headed woman suggests that his wife will turn out to be a real shrew, if she has not proved to be so already.

Ballerinas

point to the fact that deep down we are acknowledging a need for balance and poise to enter our lives.

Balloons

these long-time symbols of joy and happiness suggest that the dreamer is looking for joy and happiness of a sexual rather than a spiritual nature. However, they have also been said to suggest that hopes will be blighted and that business is heading for a downturn.

Banks

are thought to point to a need for spiritual security and on a more practical level to a growing awareness that financial affairs may need to be put on a more secure footing if the dreamer is to be able to look forward to a secure future. If the dreamer is in a bank and sees that there is no one ahead in the queue, then according to one august dream expert of days gone by, business losses loom large.

Baptism

is indicative of a new influence entering the dreamer's life and that he or she is aware that it's time to get the new broom out and start to sweep clean, especially in long-held attitudes to life. Baptism can also suggest an unspoken yet deeply felt resentment that the dreamer was forced to accept religious beliefs that are now felt to be a hindrance. It can also warn the dreamer to keep his or her opinions quiet or risk provoking an argument with friends.

Basements

and cellars are thought to represent the subconscious. When they appear in our dreams they are a signal that because we have been unable to handle things or face up to them in an adult way, we have put them to the back of our minds where they are starting to fester in some way. To dream that you are in a cold, damp cellar indicates that you are plagued with doubts. All self-confidence may well be about to evaporate like steam from a boiling kettle and you will be sunk into a deep depression from which you will find it hard to escape unless you can somehow, to put it bluntly, get a grip. Dreams of a cellar can also portend loss of property. When dreamers dream of a cellar filled with wine and stores, there is a fair chance that they will be offered a share in the profits of some sort of business venture. Before saying, 'Yes!' remember that all that glistens is not gold! Do your homework, especially into the background of whoever is putting the deal together: it may be distinctly shady! For a woman to have a similar dream is an indication that she may be about to receive an offer of marriage – from someone who is a reckless gambler!

Baskets

as long as they are full, baskets tell the dreamer that unqualified success lies ahead in anything to which the dreamer wants to turn his or her hand. But if they are empty, discontentment and sorrow cloud the horizon. To be seen trying to fill an empty basket suggests that the dreamer wants to increase his or her talents and abilities but is not sure how to go about doing so.

Bathrooms

featuring in the dream house often have one very obvious meaning – the body is trying to warn the dreamer that it's time to get up and go to the loo! Sometimes if the dreamer sees himself (and research has shown that it is more likely to be a male) passing water in his dreams, he has had a nasty accident! On a broader level, when we dream of bathrooms our subconscious is trying to tell us that there is something regarding matters of personal cleanliness that is niggling us. But for a young woman to dream of bathrooms is an indication that she is being increasingly seen as frivolous and flighty! There is one curious dream that has been dreamt by several sleepers who have reported seeing roses in the dream bathroom. The interpretation put on this by a noted interpreter is that if the flowers are white, then sickness may be about to visit the dreamer.

Baths

have a variety of meanings depending on the sex of the dreamer and the temperature of the water. If seen by a young woman she may well be increasingly afraid that other people are working against her in some way, their aim being to cause others to see her in a bad light. If the dreamer is pregnant, she should take special care, as the dream has been associated with miscarrying the baby. If the dreamer is a woman who is still in mourning for a husband who died some time before, she is being told that it is time to move on, get out more and look for new love. For a man to dream that he is in the tub is a warning that, if he is not careful, he may find himself accused of being unfaithful. Perversely, if the water is warm and relaxing, then bad things are in the offing: but if it is cold, then good health is forecast and good news is on the way. If the dreamer is sharing a bath, acquaintances may turn out to be false friends – especially if the water is not clean.

Bays

(of a topographical kind) are seen as symbolic of a woman's sexuality, the female dreamer's acceptance of it, and the male dreamer's acknowledgement that he is receptive to it. Keeping something at bay tells dreamers to keep their wits about them if they are to avoid being duped in some way. And to hear an animal baying says that the dreamer is well aware of his or her animal instincts and their willingness, indeed eagerness, to overcome them. On an equestrian level, to see oneself riding a bay mare suggests that a male dreamer will experience an upturn in fortune and that his sexual fantasies may be about to be gratified in the flesh. To the female dreamer, being atop such a mount says that her enjoyment of material things will see her giving in to the sexual advances of a predatory male.

Beaches

are an expression of the dreamer's awareness that there is a boundary between the emotional and the real and that if he or she acknowledges this when awake, life will run much more smoothly. Beaches also tell the dreamer to come down to Earth – literally, and that if he or she becomes more in tune with the elements then life will be all the better for it. Beaches can, depending on what the dreamer is doing on them and his or her state of mind at the time of the dream, indicate a need to relax more and to express the more creative side of his or her nature. If there is no one on the beach, then some interpreters see this as a sign that if the dreamer has been searching for the emotional clarity to solve a problem, the search may soon be over.

Beacons

say that the dreamer is aware that unless he makes himself aware of what is going on around him at all times, things could start to go wrong in his life. The signs that this is necessary have already been noted in the deep recesses of the mind, but have not yet registered in the conscious mind. They suggest to some interpreters that the dreamer's emotions are about to take control and lead him into dangerous waters unless they can be brought under control and the reasons acknowledged and rationalized. On another level, a beacon can be indicative of the fact that the dreamer has made the decision to let the spiritual side of life play a large part and is telling him that this was the correct decision. To seers of old, the appearance of a beacon indicated that the winds of good fortune were blowing in the dreamer's direction and that prosperity lay ahead. Beacons were also thought to say that dreamers who were suffering from ill health would soon be on the road to recovery and to businessmen that an upturn was on the cards. But to see one being extinguished or going out said that just when you thought there was plain sailing ahead, Fate had decided to have the last laugh.

Beards

often sprout in dreams. To see a beard getting longer and bushier signifies a boost to the bank balance. A non-bearded man who sees himself sporting a wispy growth on his chin should take it as a warning that he may be about to experience legal difficulties. To dream of having a beard trimmed risks a great loss of property or, worse, that he is running the risk of dying in a most unusual and unexpected way. To see one's beard being washed says that sadness lies in store. To dream that it is being pulled out by the roots is worse – great danger is lurking.

Bears

rearing up in your dreams mean that you will overwhelm any competition. Killing a bear foretells that those entangled in intricate affairs will be able to extricate themselves successfully if that is what they really want.

Bedrooms

are the places where we relax most and where most people indulge in sexual activities. To see them in a dream is an indication that we have been working too hard and need to find more time to indulge our private passions. If the linen on the bed has been freshly laundered, worries are about to fly out of the win-

29

dow. If the dreamer is a woman and she sees such a bed, a new lover may be about to make himself known to her. A dreamer who sees him or herself in bed in a room that is unfamiliar is being forewarned that friends who have not been around for some time may be about to make an unexpected and unannounced visit. For a sick person to dream of being in bed is a bad omen. Things might be about to get worse before they get better. Dreamers who see themselves asleep in an al fresco bed of some sort are being informed that good fortune is about to smile on them and will make life extremely delightful.

Beer

warns that plots are being brewed against you by those whom you had assumed to be convivial friends.

Beggars

indicate that a change in life is likely and that caution should be your watchword when dealing with strangers, for they may not be as trustworthy as they appear to be on first acquaintance.

Being barefoot

was traditionally held to warn that the dreamer's every expectation will be crushed, and that evil influences lie round every corner. Being shoeless can also be an expression of the need for sensual freedom.

Being burgled

may suggest that everyday noises have crept into the sleeper's consciousness but are not sufficiently loud to waken him or her. Freud believed the dream was caused by a fear that emotional and sexual privacy was being invaded in some way. Dream interpreters of earlier times said that if the dreamer saw himself challenging a burglar and sending him on his way it meant that a victory over enemies was within view, while to be beaten back by a burglar indicated that it was the dreamer's enemies who would emerge victorious.

Bereavement

is something that happens in all our lives and consequently occasionally turns up in our dreams. A clinical interpretation of such a dream is that while the dreamer may seem to have come to terms with a disappointment, loss or setback, the full effects have yet to make themselves apparent. In earlier times, to dream of being bereaved was thought to be a warning that long-laid plans might prove to be fruitless, no matter how successful they appeared to be at that moment. And if the dreamer sees him or herself bereft of a close relative, then such plans will definitely flounder.

Bibles

indicate that the dreamer is aware of the part that traditional moral codes can play in life and that the time has come to adopt a code of conduct that will help one mentally to survive the stress of early-twenty-first-century living. To gypsies the appearance of the Bible in a dream presaged innocent pleasure. But to be denying the teachings of the Good Book was seen as a warning that the dreamer was about to be seduced from the path of righteousness.

Biting or being bitten

has several meanings depending on who is doing the biting and what is being bitten into! Being bitten by someone we recognize tells us that we know we are the victim of some sort of aggressive behaviour but are not sure how to cope with it. Conversely, it can mean that the dreamer is not sure how to handle his or her own aggressive tendencies. To see oneself biting into something such as a fruit has a very literal interpretation: that is we should put our teeth into an opportunity that has recently presented itself. To dream of being bitten by a dog used to be thought of as a warning that quarrels with a business partner or spouse lay ahead. To be bitten by a flea said that slander was in the air and if a spider was seen to bite the dreamer, then he or she would suffer as the result of someone being unfaithful either in business or socially.

Blindness

suggests that you have put your trust in someone who will prove to be a false friend. If the dreamer owns a business of any sort, then he or she may well be let down by trusted employees. It also warns the dreamer to be extra attentive to his or her partner in life because he or she may be about to stray from the marital bed. Losing one's sight can also be a warning that affluence is about to fly out of the window, leaving the rest of one's life to be lived in abject poverty. If the dream concerns someone else's blindness, then a person the dreamer holds in some esteem will unexpectedly ask for assistance.

Boars

curiously enough don the mantle of weather-forecaster. If they root through dreams, they are indicative of stormy weather brewing. In a non-meteorological role they predict storms of a different nature being blown in by the actions of an evil-minded enemy.

Bottles

have a variety of symbolic meanings in the litany of dreams: a baby's feeding bottle points to a need to be nurtured before the dreamer's full potential can be realized. A bottle of alcohol in any form can show that there is a desire to celebrate something that has been overlooked: conversely it can warn the dreamer that there has been a little too much celebration recently and the body would like a chance to get back into balance. If the bottle is broken, it could warn that someone is about to turn to aggression to get his or her own way, or that a hoped-for success will turn out to end in failure.

Bracelets

are thought to herald marriage to a wealthy person, but not necessarily a happy marriage.

Brandy

promises wealth and distinction in the dreamer's chosen career, but that those whose good opinion they aspire to will detect a certain coarseness which will prevent them from extending the true hand of friendship to the dreamer.

Brooches

dream meanings depend on where you see yourself wearing them. If you're at home, then a friend may be about to put a business opportunity your way – and it could be a winner. But if you are wearing one in the company of strangers then you could be in danger of being robbed.

Brothers

in dreams as in life, brothers can be friend or foe! Seen active and full of energy, they say to the dreamer that good fortune is about to smile if not on the dreamer, then on someone close. If, on the other hand, the dream brother appears to be poverty stricken and asking the dreamer for help of some sort, then good fortune is about to turn her back on you, to be replaced by loss of a glum kind. More generally, dreaming about a brother is often a sign that the dreamer is becoming increasingly aware that there is some sort of uneasiness within the family and that the only way to resolve it is to bring it out into the open.

Buckles

bring bad news to female dreamers if they see themselves as having lost one, for doing so means that an important agreement that she has made or that has been made on her behalf will be broken and she will be all the worse off for it. Buckles also say that invitations are about to flood in and that in trying to cope with them all, chaos could reign – especially in business affairs.

Buffalo

stampeding through the prairies of your sleeping mind indicate that obstinate enemies are plotting against you. But diplomacy should see you victorious over them. A woman who dreams that she kills a buffalo is about to embark on a significant enterprise that, successfully completed, will bring her praise from male colleagues.

Buses

have various meanings for the dreamer. Those who see themselves sitting in a passenger seat have a strong hint that career matters are grinding to a standstill. If the dreamer is standing in a crowded bus, then competition for the next step up the career ladder will be intense. And if you see yourself going in the wrong direction, then not only are you going the wrong way in your dreams, you are going in the wrong direction in career matters. Get off the road you are on; think about what you really want to do, not what others expect you to do, and you'll be on the right track.

Cabbages

presage that a lover is wearing his or her heart on the sleeve. If those in wedlock have not yet strayed from the marital bed then they are certainly considering doing so, while those whispering words of love to an unmarried partner are simply repeating what they are also saying to another. If the dreamer is cutting the heads off cabbages. profligate expenditure will prove to be ruinous.

Cakes

are good to eat and with one exception good to dream about. They tell the dreamer that they have given their hearts to the right person and that they will inherit a house in which they will be very, very happy.

Camels

ambling across the dream landscape acknowledge the dreamer's awareness that he is being asked to bear more than his fair share of life's burdens, but that he will put up with the situation patiently until others agree to take some of the load.

Cancer

many of us think this is a modern-day problem, but it is not. It has been afflicting people for centuries and has made its presence felt in dreams for just as long. To dream that one has cancer is not a portent of ill health, but it does warn that people one loves might for no apparent reason be about to become unusually quarrelsome. And to the businessman the same dream can mean that cost-cutting measures might have to be seriously considered. To dream that cancer has been successfully treated is a sign that an upturn in the dreamer's own business or in his or her employer's will be reflected in a salary rise or bonus being paid.

Canoes

are good news – and bad. To see himself paddling a canoe across still waters is a sign that the dreamer is confident in his abilities to keep his business affairs in apple-pie order – perhaps over-confident, which could cause ripples to spread. On the roman-tic front, for a man to see himself paddling his girlfriend in a canoe is a sign that wedding invitations are about to be sent out, and that the marriage will be long and happy. But if the waters turn choppy, once wed, the bride could turn out to be hot-tem-pered. If the canoe runs aground in shallow waters, a whirlwind romance will lead to a stormy marriage. If the waters turn muddy, then the dreamer could find himself in some murky business.

Caretakers

and their modern-day equivalent, security guards, tell the dreamer that if he or she is a parent, his or her children will be unusually annoying in the near future. If you go searching for one and fail to find one, be prepared for niggling little annoy-ances that will upset your normally smooth routine. If you do find one, then strangers you meet may be so pleasant that they won't be strangers for long and could become good friends.

Carpenters

are regarded as a threat to the dreamer's composure, but it's not something to worry about – things will soon be back to normal and equanimity restored.

Carrots

tell a young woman that she will marry young and that she will give birth to a string of bonny babies that will live long, healthy lives. To other dreamers, carrots indicate that prosperity and health can be taken for granted.

Cats

worshipped by the Ancient Egyptians as gods, feared by those who believe in such things as a witch's link to the Devil, cats bring different messages as they pad elegantly through our dreams. To be scratched by a cat is an unlucky portent, to be nuzzled by one suggests that treachery and deceit are on the cards. To kill one suggests that the dreamer will triumph over his enemies. If the dream cat is black, then beware. Unlike its living counterpart, which is a symbol of good luck to the awake in many parts of the world, such a cat suggests that evil in some shape or form is about to take shape. Kittens on the other hand are symbolic of joy and peace and harmony in the home. But if the little cat unsheathes its claws and scratches you, then marital harmony will be hard to find.

Cattle

a symbol of wealth in many parts of the world, cattle bring the same meaning to the dreamer. On its own, a cow symbolizes Mother Earth and may indicate that the dreamer has a yet-unacknowledged desire to return to a simpler life than is at present being lived. A bull seen in dreams is usually taken as an erotic symbol and many interpreters suggest that its appearance means that a male dreamer is aware subconsciously that in matters of personal sexuality, all is not as it seems. A bull bellowing in a woman's dream may be the subconscious telling the dreamer that her sex-life could be improved.

Cedar trees

with their well-known shape and height, distinctive perfume and healing qualities should, if things were what they seem on the dream landscape, denote that happiness, joy and peace are about to wrap themselves round the dreams. And for once, the obvious is the actual.

Celery

suggests that dreams of prosperity will not only be achieved, they will be far surpassed. Eating it alone says that love will warm you for as long as you live. For a girl to dream of eating it with her lover signifies she will inherit considerable wealth.

Cemeteries

with their obvious associations with death have a double, indeed treble, psychological significance. They can represent parts of the dreamer that he has discarded or that he has simply stopped using, either knowingly or unknowingly, something that was once an important part of his being. They can also, perhaps more obviously, signify that the dreamer is increasingly aware of his mortality and his attitude towards it. A third interpretation is that when cemeteries appear in our dreams, we are giving ourselves permission to show our fear of something, not necessarily death, important to us. On a more fanciful level, to see an immaculately well-kept cemetery, its gravestones free from weeds and with its grassy areas neatly trimmed, presages that someone you have given up for dead (perhaps not physically but with whom there had been no contact for such a long time that he or she has been forgotten) is about to reappear in your life. Romanies believed that to see such a dream signifies that property that had been lost to a usurper was about to be returned. And continuing with such interpretations, to see an ill-tended cemetery means that the dreamer will live to see loved ones desert him and leave him to spend his final years in the care of strangers. But for young people to see themselves strolling along line after line of gravestones is thought to signify that their friends would be a great source of comfort to them in times of sorrow which are, sadly, unavoidable. Engaged women who saw themselves being married in a dream cemetery were, in days gone by, believed to be being warned that their spouses (when they eventually married them) would meet a fatal accident while on a journey far from home. Good news, though, for married women to dream they are walking through a burial ground clasping a large bunch of flowers. Gypsies believed (and still do) that such a dream was a sign that family members were destined to enjoy robust good health all of their lives. And for women in mourning for their dead husbands to dream of being in a cemetery presaged that black clothes would soon be exchanged for some of a colour more suited to a woman being married a second time! Two pieces of good news are heralded by dreams of cemeteries. First for older people: if burial places feature in your dreams, then especially pleasant journeys lie ahead at the end of which you will be perfectly rested and invigorated. Second, dreaming of young children picking flowers from a graveyard was traditionally regarded as a sign that the winds of prosperity were about to blow in the dreamer's direction.

Chairs

tell the dreamer that there is an obligation that is due to be met but for some reason there is a reluctance on the dreamer's part to do this. But if the right action is not taken and duties fulfilled as promised, a significant loss may result. To dream of a friend sitting quite motionless on a chair is a sign that he or she might be about to be hit by a bout of ill health – and one that could be serious.

Chandeliers

if they are in sparkling condition, chandeliers tell the dreamer to set his sights high for what seems absolutely unobtainable at present is there for the taking if he puts his mind to it. On the other hand, if the chandelier is broken or in need of a good clean, then beware of investing in a speculative venture. It will end not just in tears but in significant financial loss. And if the lights flicker and go out, what seems to be a promising future will be clouded by disappointment.

Chameleons

charm those who watch them with their ability to change their colour to match the background. In dreams, sadly, they point to the fact that someone is being cheated mercilessly by an acquaintance. And that someone is the dreamer.

Cherubs

say that the dreamer is going to go through a particularly happy phase in his or her life, the memory of which will stay forever. That is, if they are smiling beatifically. If they are frowning or in any other way looking displeased, then the dreamer is about to hear some particularly depressing news.

Children

seen in dreams remind us that there are parts of us that are, and probably always will be, childish. When we recognize this we are well on the way to becoming more rounded people, so when children feature in our dreams, it may well be the subconscious's way of telling the dreamer that the time for that recognition has come. They are generally regarded as being a positive image, especially if they are in obvious good health and playing happily. It is hardly surprising that children, not necessarily the dreamer's own offspring, feature often in the dreams of parents when you think of how large they feature in adults' lives, their capacity to cause problems, their capacity to surprise and their capacity to bring unparalleled joy into life. If it is one's own offspring seen in a dream it is thought to be a good sign, suggesting that the immediate future will be especially cheerful. For a mother to dream that she has many beautiful children is a sign that many blessings will be brought to her by her offspring. If the dream concerns a child who has had a minor accident, she will be upset by lots of little niggles – nothing serious, but annoying all the same. If the child is hard at work at his or her books, a period of prosperous calm is heralded. To dream of a child stricken by illness suggests that its welfare (not necessarily its health) is under threat. And although dreams of a dead child may be extremely upsetting, they don't forewarn the child's death, but rather that worrying or disappointing news is in the offing. If the child is seen as being disappointed, perhaps crying or frowning, then acquaintances who appear to be friendly are, in fact, being duplicitous.

Churchyards

have three main meanings. First the bad news! To dream of strolling through one that is covered with a coating of snow crisp underfoot denotes that if poverty is to be avoided, a huge effort will have to be made. In avoiding penury, the dreamer may have to leave family and friends behind and go and live far away – at least for a little while. Next the not quite so bad news. If the dreamer is female, in love and sees herself in a churchyard it is an indication that she and her love will never share the marital bed with each other and that true happiness lies with someone else. Now for the good news: if spring is obviously in the air then friends will make life especially pleasant in the immediate future and the opportunity to travel to new, exciting and extremely beautiful places is about to present itself.

Clocks

alert the dreamer to the passage of time, perhaps to an awakening of mortality, or maybe they signify an awareness that the time is right to do something that we have been putting off doing and which has now become urgent.

Closeness

in the physical rather than the weather sense suggests that the dreamer is growing increasingly aware that there is a need for intimacy and/or protection. If this is not satisfied in the near future, then the dreamer will become more and more afraid that the future will be lonely and perhaps unsafe.

Clover

a traditional symbol of good luck in life, clover is just as lucky in dreams, where it signifies that Dame Fortune is arranging things to the dreamer's benefit. To dream of it in any of its many-leafed varieties can also suggest that the dreamer is concerned that the various parts that go to make up his whole are out of tune with each other and that for harmony to be restored the scales must be rebalanced.

Clubs

of the sort which our prehistoric ancestors used as weapons are seen as symbolic of violence lying deep within us. This has probably been dormant and unexpressed for years, perhaps since childhood, but is now surfacing in the dreamer's subconscious and may be about to make its presence felt in the waking as well as the sleeping life. Clubs can also say that the dreamer harbours violent feelings about something for which he has never been able to forgive himself. They can also say that the dreamer possesses enormous strength which has yet to be channelled properly. In the social sense, clubs indicate the desire that we all have to belong. If we see ourselves as having a good time and mixing well with others then it's probable that we see ourselves as part of society as a whole. But if we are lingering like wallflowers at the back of the border, then this suggests that we see ourselves as being separate from our peers, and that we are not sure why this should be. However, like all problems, the solution or part of it lies in recognizing that there is a problem in the first place. Once the dreamer acknowledges this, he or she can take the appropriate steps in order to remedy it.

Coffins

are a reminder that everyone is mortal and that the dreamer is no exception. They also say that he or she is coming to terms with some sort of loss, perhaps the death of a relationship that was once central to the dreamer's life. They can also suggest that the dreamer is cutting off certain feelings and in doing so is allowing part of him or herself to die. For centuries, coffins have been seen as unlucky dream symbols. For farmers they were thought to warn of failed harvests and poor livestock, while to businessmen they were seen as a warning that debts were about to mount up and go out of control. To young dreamers, coffins warned that marital happiness was unlikely to be theirs, at least not with their present partners! If the dreamer saw his or her own coffin, then there was gloom on both the domestic and the business fronts. And to see oneself sitting on a coffin was thought to be a warning that illness of a non-fatal nature was about to strike the dreamer.

Cold

signifies neglect in the dream dictionary. To see oneself as being cold suggests that the dreamer feels left out of things.

Combs

tidy our hair in our waking hours and when seen in dreams suggest that there is an as yet unacknowledged need to tidy up some aspect of our lives. Maybe it's our jobs that we need to pay some attention to, or a relationship that has gone a bit straggly at the edges and needs straightening out.

Comets

flashing across a dream warn that the dreamer is afraid that there is a situation brewing which he or she knows will be impossible to control. What is going to happen is going to happen no matter what the dreamer does, so the only thing to do is prepare for the eventual flak, regardless of the direction in which it is scattered. That's one interpretation. Another is that the dreamer is puzzling over how to solve a problem and that the dream tells him that he should look for a practical solution rather than rely on a flash of inspiration.

Compasses

suggest that the dreamer needs help in charting his way through the immediate future. They often appear when the dreamer has been presented with a set of choices and has no idea which one or ones to select. Another meaning that has been laid at compasses' door is that the dreamer feels that he or she has been the victim of some injustice and this is starting to impinge on rational thought when awake.

Computers

(curse or blessing according to the dreamers' experiences of them) are new on the dream landscape, the first electronic one having been developed within the comparatively recent past. Interpreters are still not quite keyed in to their true meaning, but there is a growing consensus that they indicate that the dreamer is slowly coming round to the idea that he or she has untapped resources that could add to material and spiritual wellbeing. They may also suggest that every experience we have ever gone through since the moment we were born (maybe even since the moment when the first brain cells developed in the foetus) has been stored and is there to be rediscovered and evaluated.

Conch shells

with their beautiful spiral shape and luminescent linings lend themselves to ideas of perfection in real life. In dreams they suggest that the dreamer is gradually becoming aware that life need not be as dull as a 1950s Scottish Sunday and that a little Saturday Night Fever is good for the spirits. Some societies in which the conch shell was (and may still be) used as a trumpet think that to dream of one serves as a warning of some kind. They may be right. And with that in mind, perhaps the dreamer who sees one should remember the old maxim, 'Forewarned is forearmed.'

Cooking

can tell the dreamer that he or she has a hunger that is demanding to be satisfied – not necessarily a physical hunger, perhaps an emotional one or a craving to make use of opportunities that have presented themselves but that have been sidelined for the time being. To see oneself as cooking can be the subconscious's way of telling the dreamer to take such opportunities out of the shunting yard and get them back on the rails before it's too late. To be preparing food can also be the mind's way of telling the dreamer that he or she has all the ingredients for success and that if only the right recipe is found, the future can be faced with increased confidence.

Corners

need to be turned in dreams as well as in life, and when we see ourselves going round one, it is probable that we are congratulating ourselves for having surmounted some obstacles and coming through as stronger, more capable people. If, however, we see ourselves approaching one in our dreams, then it indicates that there is a problem coming up. If it is a left-handed one, then the answer to it probably lies in using intuition rather than acting logically. If the corner is right-handed, then the dreamer should follow logic rather than emotion to get round it. Corners can also suggest that the dreamer has been living a lie for some time – not necessarily a thundering whopper, maybe just a tiny white one. The dream says that the dreamer is coming close to acknowledging that the time is right to come clean or else he or she will feel trapped in a web of deceit for ever. Anyone in this situation who sees a corner coming up or being turned should remember that you can fool all of the people some of the time and you can fool some of the people all of the time. But you cannot fool all of the people all of the time.

Corpses

have a variety of meanings. The most common interpretation, especially among sages of days gone by, is an obvious one that when a corpse appears in a dream, the sad – very sad – news will be received concerning an absent friend. For businessmen such a dream warns that the good times may be over – for ever. And to young dreamers, corpses herald that the immediate future is unlikely to be marked by happiness! If the dead body is being placed in a coffin by the undertaker's men, it suggests imminent unspecified troubles for the dreamer. Lovers dreaming of dead bodies is thought to be a sure sign that promises made will turn out to be promises broken. If the corpse is animal rather than human, then the dreamer's health is under threat – though not necessarily physical health: it is perhaps to spiritual or financial health that the dreamer should turn his or her attention.

Couches

when seen with the dreamer lounging on them, couches say that hopes may take wing but that they will crash land almost as soon as they have taken off! They warn the dreamer to be especially careful in business matters for if there is the slightest loss of concentration, the effect could be out of all proportion to the cause.

Cradles

dreamt of occupied by a bonny baby tell the dreamer that if things turn out as planned, prosperity is theirs for the taking and that if they have children, the offspring will do their parents proud and stay friends with them throughout their lives. But if a young mother sees herself rocking her own baby in a cradle, another member of the family could be about to come down with an illness of some sort. If a childless, unmarried woman dreams that she is rocking a cradle she should keep her ears open for tittle-tattle that may be being spread about her.

Cranes

(the ones seen on building sites rather than the feathered variety) tell the dreamer that it is time to raise awareness about something that has been lurking in the dark recesses of the mind for some time. It's likely that the dreamer has been focusing on distracting detail – the dream tells him that it's time to see the bigger picture. They also say that if he puts his mind to something, he should be able to put himself in the driving seat and turn a situation to his advantage.

Crowds

suggest that the dreamer is unwilling to be singled out for any one attribute and would prefer to stay in the background, out of the limelight in most aspects of life. That may be all right for some, but it could suggest an irresponsible attitude to life. If the crowd is well dressed and perhaps enjoying some sort of entertainment, pleasant times lie ahead in the company of convivial friends. But if anything happens to mar the crowd's enjoyment, then friendship may be about to desert the dreamer's life to be replaced by unhappiness. The change in mood can also indicate dissent in the family. If the crowd is in a street then the dreamer's business will perk up and prosperity beckons. If the dreamer is shouting to make himself heard above the noise of a crowd, he may find himself standing accused of pushing his own interests above those of others. According to Jung, an outwardly calm person who dreamed of a crowd was, deep down, in a state of some agitation!

Daggers

when seen being used offensively by the dreamer suggest he or she harbours a desire to cut something out of his or her life, which has come to be seen as redundant. If the weapon is being used against the dreamer, then it is likely that a feeling of vulnerability is being acknowledged.

Daisies

may be a nightmare for gardeners in search of the perfect lawn, but if they show their pretty heads in spring or summer dreams they suggest that a true lover is about to present him or herself. Sadly, if daisies show themselves in winter or autumn dreams, the looming lover will turn out to be wearing his heart on his sleeve.

Dams

tell dream analysts that emotions are being bottled up and could break through at any time, causing devastating effect on the dreamer's life. They can also suggest that the dreamer suspects that someone else may be about to let his emotions fly in the dreamer's direction and that he or she would prefer that this did not happen. To be seen building a dam is indicative that the dreamer is shoring up his defences lest some hurt be about to upset his equilibrium. And if a dam is seen to burst, then the dreamer is expressing a fear that he or she knows no way in which to control the emotions of close members of the family.

Dancing

is a happy dream with a happy message. Married dreamers who see children tripping the light fantastic will be blessed with a happy home life and a large family. Younger people who dream of dancing can expect a smooth path through life for the immediate future. If you dream that you are being taught to dance, there will be a strong temptation to neglect business and pursue insignificant pleasures: do not give into them, for if you do, the outcome could be disastrous. Different sorts of dances have slightly different meanings, but as most of them signify pleasant activities and good companionship, they do not have to be looked at individually – unless the dreamer is a woman and she is waltzing with her lover, for she will change partners many times in her life but never find true happiness with any of them.

Dandelions

warn that someone you trust and who may be working with you on a project that is close to your heart has perfidiousness inscribed on his.

Darkness

warns that in the immediate future work will not go well. But if the sun breaks through, things will pick up very soon. If the dream concerns searching for someone in the dark, then you will be provoked by trivialities into losing your temper with dramatic results. Keep your cool and you should be OK. Lose it and look out! If you dream that you are groping around in a strange place in the dark, then you may be about to get an urgent summons to somewhere you have never been before where sorrow of some kind waits to welcome you.

Daughters

when seen in a dream, daughters suggest that there are stormy times blowing in but that, as with the weather, nothing lasts for ever, and the storm-force winds will die down to be replaced by calm and pleasant times.

Daughters-in-law

often have uncomfortable relationships with their husbands' mothers, and when they feature in a dream they signify that some unusual event is about to occur. If the offspring's wife is smiling and happy then something unusually nice is heralded. If she is scowling and glum then something unusually nasty might be round the corner.

Dawns

are as welcome in dreams as they are after long, dark nights, as long as they are bright and clear, for they say that business is set for success and the dreamer can look forward to the immediate future with confidence. But if the sky is overcast, then dull routine will wear the dreamer down to the point that life becomes a drudge.

Days

when they appear in the dreamer's sleeping mind, days herald an all-round boost in life: business will go well, job prospects will pick up and any hints of disharmony on the home front will vanish. Unless, that is, the day is gloomy and overcast, for in that case a new enterprise that looked promising will prove the old saying that all that glistens is not gold!

Death

is perhaps one of the most common subjects of dreams – whether it be the dreamer or another person who is seen to shuffle off the coils of mortal life. To dream of seeing a member of the family dead is a warning that the dreamer's increasingly dissolute way of life is being talked about among relations and friends. Such dreams are often followed by disappointment of some sort. If, in the dream, the death is heard about rather than seen, then bad news is on its way.

Decorating

a house suggests that the dreamer is increasingly aware that personal relationships have fallen into disrepair and that fences need to be mended.

Deer

running through a dream, according to gypsy folklore, presage that disputes with one's sweetheart are in the offing. And if the deer in question is a fawn, then the quarrel will be about the other's inconsistency. To dream of killing a deer makes it likely that you will receive an inheritance from an old man – if the deer in question is a hart, likelihood turns to certainty – and that the deceit of an unknown enemy is about to be exposed. If the hart is running fleet-footed through the dream, then wealth is about to be offered, but it will be achieved through subtle rather than obvious means.

Demolition

has been reported surprisingly often as a dream theme. Its meaning depends on who is doing the demolishing. If it's the dreamer, then he or she is expressing a need to be in control in most situations. The dreamer is often the sort of person who seems to be driven by ambition, but is impossible to work with unless he (and the dreamer is usually a male) is in the boss's chair. If someone else is doing the demolishing, then the dreamer is acknowledging his awareness that other people control the most important elements of his life, and if there are to be changes, no matter how unpleasant, there is little the dreamer feels can be done about them.

Desks

seen being used by dreamers suggest that bad luck may roll down on them. But if there are coins or banknotes on the surface, then dreamers who have been having financial problems may find that an unexpected windfall, maybe in the form of a bonus or a win of some sort, is about to help ease things.

Devouring

In devouring dreams people often see themselves as being devoured by something or someone, as opposed to enjoying a burger and fries! When the former is experienced, the dreamer is expressing a deeply rooted but unexpressed fear of losing his or her identity because of developing some sort of obsession.

Diamonds

signify that those in positions of authority will smile at you and nudge you up the ladder of success at every opportunity. If a young woman dreams that an admirer is giving her diamonds then she should stick with him for he will do well and marriage to him would ensure a comfortable and prosperous life. But if the dream concerns losing diamonds then disgrace is waiting to welcome the dreamer in the not too distant future. That's what one source suggests. Others put different interpretations on dream diamonds. To pick up a dropped diamond may mean loss or sorrow, while to be offered one on a plate signifies wealth success and happiness. And another claims that wearing diamonds might indicate that the dreamer will be mixed up in some gossip that will lead to serious trouble, perhaps even loss of employment.

Dictators

be they well known tyrants such as Hitler or Stalin, or an autocratic and overbearing boss perhaps, feature in the dreams of those who have been brought up by extremely strict parents. When they are dreamed, such dictators may be saying the dreamer is still concerned that he or she is still not living up to the standards that the parents set, or that the child has disappointed the parents in some other way.

Diving

when the water is clear tells the dreamer that any embarrassment that has been rippling around him will soon be a thing of the past. Making a splash in muddied waters, however, signifies that the dreamer is increasingly aware that life in general and business in particular may be about to take a turn for the worse. To see others enjoying diving says that the dreamer will be surrounded by good companions. And for lovers to dream that they are diving together tells them that they can look forward to a long life together and that the flames of passion will never cool.

Doctors

are seen to carry good news in their bags when they pay a call in the sleeper's dreams. Often seen as authority figures, they can presage that the dreamer is seen to be doing well at work and has been marked out for promotion. They can, of course, suggest that the dreamer is worried about his or her health and is about to acknowledge that whatever may be the matter should be referred to a professional physician.

Dogs

are one of the most popularly dreamed of animals. It's the way the dog behaves rather than the individual breed that is significant. That said, bulldogs suggest that the dreamer is blessed with a wide circle of loyal friends. To dream of hounds, be they fox, stag or any other type, warns the dreamer that schemes being laid will end with no profit being made. If the dog, any dog, is friendly, then the dreamer can depend on friends to help out in times of need. If it is snappy on the other hand, it may be that betrayal may be about to be experienced. And to be bitten by a dog is symbolic of suffering from an injury at the hands of a friend.

Dolphins

long seen as friends on hand to sailors in distress, dolphins tell the dreamer that he or she may be about to be plunged into unexpected adventures. But if the dolphin is seen floundering out of water, then it could be that a sweetheart or a friend is about to disappear from the picture.

Donkeys and mules

are known for their patient endurance. It is appropriate then that to dream of them suggests that patience is the virtue required for overcoming an obstacle standing in the dreamer's path. If the beasts are behaving badly, snapping and biting, then the dreamer should beware a member of their household behaving in an underhand manner.

Doorbells

whether they are heard or being rung in a dream, doorbells warn that your routine is about to be abruptly disrupted by a summons to attend to an urgent business matter or to the bedside of an ailing relative.

Doors

have many meanings in the dream dictionary. Many psychologists believe that they represent the body's openings, and therefore the dreamer's sexuality. Opening and closing doors can indicate the dreamer's attitude to sex and sexuality, while refusing to open a door can be symptomatic of a childish approach to sex. To be seen barring a door suggests that the dreamer is searching for self-protection. Dreaming of doors can suggest that the dreamer is willing to present a more approachable face to society. But it can also suggest that in appearing more approachable, the dreamer might be worried that he or she will appear to be seen as being more vulnerable and that others may take advantage of this. To dream of breaking a door down tells the dreamer that now is the time to tackle any inhibitions that have been holding him back, especially in sexual matters. To dream of going through one suggests that you are trying to escape the slanders that vituperative tongues are casting in your direction. There is an exception: if the door you are entering is one that you remember from your childhood home, then good times are on the other side. Dreaming of coming out of the rain and going through a door at night suggests, to a female dreamer, that she has been up to something of which she is deeply ashamed. To a male, the same dream signifies that he is about to have to draw on his resources to pay for his (as yet unknown) vices! To see others going through a door tells the dreamer that he or she is going to have to work extremely hard to straighten out their financial affairs. To see a door fall off its hinges and injure someone after you have been trying to close it is a warning that some advice you have given him or her will cause them unhappiness or bad luck. To see someone try to lock a door and then to see it become unhinged says that you will hear that a friend has or is about to come unstuck in some way and that you are or will be powerless to help them.

Draughts

are an indication that the dreamer is aware of being in a position where external forces over which he or she has little control could be about to blow the winds of change through their lives. Draughts are often reported in the dreams of those who work in industries or businesses that are unusually susceptible to sudden changes in market forces and where having what seems to be a very secure job on a Monday is no guarantee that a redundancy cheque won't be paid into the bank by Friday. To be seen to be creating a draught on the other hand suggests that the dreamer is the type of person who will always act as peacemaker when disputes threaten to ruffle feathers.

Dressing

in a dream suggests that you have recently done something of which you are not feeling at all proud and would prefer to keep to yourself.

Droughts

are not to be welcomed during our sleeping hours! Family squabbles will deepen into serious arguments that could take some time to settle. Droughts also herald ill health heading the dreamer's way and that plans that looked as if they had been built on firm foundations will turn out to be have been built on shifting sands! Farmers used to dread dreaming of drought because according to rural folklore, such a dream served as a warning that some of their livestock may be about to meet with a fatal accident.

Drunkenness

can be a good thing or a bad thing: it depends upon what the dreamer has been drinking! If spirits are the cause of your inebriation beware, for your reputation for overindulgence may well be about to cost you your job. Having drunk too much wine, on the other hand, is good news, especially for those who have literary ambitions, for this dream presages success in that direction.

Dusk

says that hopes are about to be dashed on the rocks of disappointment – especially if they concern business or career. Unmarried women who are seeing someone 'on the side' and who dream that they are walking hand in hand with their paramours in the dusk can wave goodbye to secrecy! Their secret is about to be blown.

Ears

warn you to listen out for rumours that someone you know and trust is playing a waiting game, watching your every move until there is a hiccup in business matters or squabble in the home. He or she will then do everything to make sure that the blame is heaped on you and in doing so show themselves in a better light.

Earthquakes

used to be regarded as a sign that nation would make war unto nation! Today, they are more likely to denote business failure. If your house is seen to shake during an earthquake, then some sort of official announcement could be about to affect your property. To married women, dream earthquakes are thought to herald good news. But to dream of an earthquake when there may have been a little hiccup in the workplace suggests that a jealous colleague caused it. And if the land is seen to split during an earthquake, then according to one sage of the dim and distant past, you could be in danger of becoming trapped in a fire.

Eclipses

solar eclipses are indicative that the dreamer holds deep-rooted fears about the direction life is taking and is concerned that success may always be elusive. Colleagues and friends, the dreamer thinks, seem to have achieved some degree of importance because they give an impression of being more able than he is, something that prevents him from showing his true potential. Eclipses also often feature in dreams at times when the dreamer is putting a brave face on things and feels that this may not be possible for much longer. Dream interpreters of the past thought that to dream of an eclipse served as a warning that the dreamer should mend his ways and curb his excesses if his health was not to suffer. A lunar eclipse, on the other hand, said that if the dreamer could keep his head when all around were losing theirs, he would be unaffected by an oncoming unpleasantness.

Education

with its obvious connection to school and university, education says to dreamers that the time has come to be more disciplined than they have been of late if they are not to be seen to be performing inadequately either in career or family matters. It also says that lessons learnt in the past, if applied to the present and future, could provide considerable benefits. On a more superficial level, to dream of education could indicate that the dreamer sees a better education as the key to success. Ninety-nine times out of a hundred, this could be true, but there's always that one percent!

Eggs

are thought to be symbolic of the dreamer's awareness that there are huge reserves of potential that have still to be tapped. They also say that before he or she can enjoy life to the full, part of which can only be achieved if that potential is fully realized, planning will be all-important. And as part of this planning progress, the dreamer may have to withdraw, monk-like, into the cell of his own mind for a while and emerge, butterfly-like as a new being. Fortune-tellers of old believed that to dream of a nest of eggs was a sign that financial gains were in view. If the eggs were small, the windfall would be similarly tiny but would come at a time of great need and would still be seen as a blessing. And if the eggs were cracked, the good fortune would drift out of the dreamer's life to be replaced by disappointment whereas bright, shiny eggs herald-ed a happy event in the family.

Electricity

unknown to sages two centuries ago, electricity is a compara-tively recent arrival on the dream stage. With its associations with power, it says to the dreamer that we all have the power to make a contribution to life and it is up to us to find out what it is. If we grab it, we just may leave a footstep in the sands of time, but if we let it slip from our grasp, our lives will go unmarked by future generations. If the dreamer sees himself as being electrocuted or suffering an electric shock he is being told to be on the alert if he is not to fall victim to some sort of danger.

Elephants

are a good omen. To see yourself surveying the world from a howdah, atop an elephant's back, indicates that significant, solid wealth will trundle your way and that honours, which you will wear with suitable dignity, will be bestowed on you. Business colleagues and family alike will accept whatever you say with the utmost respect. If a herd of those wondrous beasts fills your dreams, then the wealth coming your way will be very significant. If you dream that you are feeding an elephant, your efforts to help the community in which you live will be recognized and suitably rewarded.

Escape

tells us that the dreamer is keen to avoid a difficult situation about to present itself, or wants to move on from one that has already arrived. It may be that the dreamer is in a position of some responsibility which he is finding onerous and would like to relinquish. Some dream interpreters think that the escape dream is most often experienced by people who found their childhood so intolerable that they have spent their adult lives trying to leave it behind, but are constantly haunted by their demons. Gypsies believed, and still do, that to dream of escaping from jail meant a rapid rise up the career ladder, while to escape from the clutches of a wild animal suggested that the dreamer should be on the alert lest the schemes of a false friend land him in trouble.

Evenings

suggest that hopes and plans that the dreamer has come to think would never be realized will suddenly be back on the agenda and will come to happy fulfilment. If there are stars shining in the evening sky, then there may be trouble ahead, but if you face the music and dance, you'll soon put it behind you. But to see yourself walking hand in hand with your lover in the evening twilight is a suggestion that night may be about to fall on your relationship – for a short while at least.

Eyes

are not to be welcomed, warning as they do that enemies are on the lookout for the slightest chance to make mischief, either in business affairs or in matters of the heart. If it's the former, then whoever is plotting will use extremely devious ways to achieve his ends. If it's the latter, then a rival is just biding his time before trying to worm his way into a sweetheart's regard. And in both cases, if the dreamer is not careful, the loss will be theirs. If the colour of the dream eyes is striking, then the colour itself is more significant than the eye. Brown eyes warn that deceit is all around. Blue eyes suggest that while the dreamer has good intentions, the willpower to see them to fruition is probably lacking. Grey eyes suggest that their owner is open to flattery.

Fables

can indicate several things to the dream interpreter. They can say that dull labour is a thing of the past and that the future is filled with pleasant duties. They can also suggest that the dreamer has a talent for writing that has not so far been exploited. If the fables dreamed of are religious in nature, then the dreamer may be slowly awakening to the fact that the spiritual side of life has been neglected. To dream of being part of a fable is to be warned that there is too much pretence in the dreamer's life and that ostrich-like he has his head buried in the sand. It is time, the dream is saying, to wake up and face the truth about something, no matter how unpleasant it may be. And to dream of fabulous beasts such as unicorns suggests that the dreamer has been trying to reconcile two sides of an argument – and has failed to do so.

Failure

of a personal nature is dreamed of by people of a highly competitive nature who fear that they are being seen by their peers as performing inadequately – not necessarily in the workplace, but more often than not in the bedroom. If the dream recurs then the dreamer is being warned that this fear of failure is clouding all his judgement. Dreamers who experience this should come to understand that we can't be successful all the time and that into every life a little failure must fall.

Fainting

is a warning that illness may be about to hit your family or that you may receive bad news about someone you haven't heard from for some time. If the dreamer is a woman and she sees herself falling into a deep faint, then she should mend her ways because her carelessness might well be about to be the cause of a deep disappointment. Fainting in a dream can also indicate that someone you trust is about to let you down.

Fakirs

are not especially common, but noteworthy nonetheless for their suggestion that many changes lie in store. They also suggest that the dreamer is aware on a subconscious level that friends who have offered to help in some way have yet to put their money where their mouths are – and perhaps never will.

Fame

suggests that the dreamer is a shrinking violet when it comes to recognizing his or her own abilities. Deep down, of course, dreamers know what their true potential is, and to see themselves as famous in their dreams is compensation for their failure to achieve it in real life. Gypsy tradition holds that to dream of being famous is to be warned to expect some sort of reversal, especially in business.

Fathers

traditionally underline that parent's love for their dreaming child and are a sign that they will always be there for their children. But they have other meanings, too. Sometimes, to dream of your father suggests that a difficulty of some sort lies ahead and that you will need some very good advice (perhaps from a legal expert) if you are to extricate yourself from it. If the dead father appears in a dream, it could be that there are business difficulties ahead and you may have to put the brakes on a deal you were keen to go ahead with. If the dreamer is a young woman and she dreams that her father is dead, she should keep an eye on her boyfriend or husband because he may be having an affair.

Films

seen in dreams can be quite spooky – a bit like watching a play within a play. One interpretation of them is that the dreamer is aware that something belonging to the past needs to be taken off the shelf, dusted down and reinterpreted if he is to really come to terms with its effect on his life. To dream of sitting in the director's chair or peering down the viewfinder of a movie camera (when one is not a movie director or a film cameraman!) is a suggestion that the life the dreamer is making for himself is not based in reality. To succeed, foundations will have to be dug deeper than they are at present.

Fire

says that prosperity will warm your life, even if it is engulfing your home, when it foretells that your choice of partner was, or will be, an excellent one and that your children will be as obedient as any children ever are. If the fire is spreading through the dreams of a businessman and burning down his shop or office, then the order books will soon be bursting and a period of prolonged prosperity will be enjoyed. But if he is fighting the fire and is unscathed, then the workload will become heavier than it has been of late, and there may be hiccups in the smooth running of the business. And if dreamers see themselves standing in the smouldering ruins of their business then such is the bad luck in store that they will be tempted to call it a day. However, they shouldn't despair, for a totally unexpected stroke of good fortune will soon have them back on their feet again. If the fire is of a domestic nature, and the dream concerns sitting by the fireside, kindling the coals, then an unexpected visit from some long unseen friends is about to happen.

Fire engines

racing to an emergency, lights blazing and sirens wailing, warn that the dreamer is about to be hit by some totally unexpected event that will see fortune not so much smiling but positively beaming on the dreamer. But if they are seen by an unmarried woman, her behaviour may be about to be called into question. Some dreamers have taken the appearance of a fire engine in their dreams as a warning to make sure their fire insurance is in order – and have been glad that they did so!

Fireworks

when cascading through a woman's dream, fireworks presage travel to somewhere she has never been before and that the trip will be an exceptionally pleasant one. To dreamers of either sex, they indicate good health and a sunny time ahead. More specifically, if the firework is a Roman candle then you will achieve what you want in the immediate future, but if the firework fizzles out, then so too will the ambition.

Floods

are as disastrous to the dreamer as they can be in real life, for to dream that you are being swept along in a flood that is destroying huge areas of the country is to be warned that your health is about to go on a downward slope. Not just that, your business could be heading for the rocks along with your marriage! If the flood turns into what can only be called an inundation of dirty water, then that suggests a bereavement. But if the water is clear, then after a spell when the dreamer thinks that things just can't get worse, he's quite right. They will pick up and the waters of despair will recede to be replaced by the rays of bright sunshine. An old interpretation of dreaming of floods was that people richer than the dreamer will cause him problems and it could be that a wealthy rival in love is about to steal a march on him.

Flowers

can be difficult to define when they feature in dreams. They have great individual meanings in astrology, aromatherapy and other New Age studies, but in dreams they seem to merge into one great bouquet. Obvious interpretations involve romance, but this is far too easy. Wild flowers provide the best omens, often suggesting impending sexual encounters. If these don't happen they still suggest only pleasant adventures. Generally speaking – if one can talk generalities in the dream context – flowers are symbolic of beauty, love and tenderness. Of course, they have sexual connotations: a blossoming flower is symbolic of female genitalia, a bud of the male sexual organ. If the flowers dreamed of are in season, joy may be about to flood into the dreamer's life, unless the flowers are white in which case the joy may be short lived, or yellow, which presages difficulties of some sort, or red – in which case death may be about to shroud a loved one.

Football

is a difficult dream to interpret as despite its long history, its surge in popularity has been comparatively recent. Most current dream interpreters consider that to dream of football is to suggest that the dreamer is living with his head in the clouds when, if he is to do anything with his life, he should make sure his feet are planted firmly on the ground.

Friends

can have an obvious meaning in dreams. If a friend has been in our thoughts, then he or she is quite liable to pop up in the dream world at any time. But of course, they have a deeper meaning. If we dream of the same friend over and over again, then perhaps the subconscious is suggesting that the time has come to examine the friendship and what it really means to us. It may be that we have come to see the person as being rather more than a friend, or that friendship has slipped to the Christmas card level and the dreamer must decide whether or not to make the conscious effort to revive it, or to let it become a pleasant acquaintanceship rather than a true friendship. On a slightly more fanciful level, the appearance of good friends in a dream heralds good news concerning either them or a close relative. If the friends dreamed of appear to be especially friendly, then current activities will be particularly successful. If, however, the friends are sad or unhappy, then you can expect to receive news that someone of your acquaintance has been stricken with illness.

Funerals

warn of an unhappy marriage and that any offspring will be puny and whingy children who, if they survive into adulthood, will be puny and whingy adults! That is if the person being buried is known to the dreamer: if not then the interment denotes that unexpected worries are about to descend. If a woman sees herself as dressed in black and following a funeral cortege, then according to gypsy belief any fears she has of early widowhood will come true. And if parents of either sex

66

see themselves attending the funeral of one or other of their children, a friend with good intentions will raise hopes high only to dash them on the rocks of disappointment shortly afterwards. On a deeper level, to dream of being at a funeral is thought to be an indication that the dreamer needs to come to terms with their attitude towards death. It can also indicate that the time has come to bury memories of some sad or disappointing event and move on. And to dream of one's own funeral suggests that the dreamer feels that he deserves sympathy for something and feels disappointed that it is not forthcoming. And before the subject is buried, to dream of one's parent's death is an indication that the dreamer feels that it is time to assert his or her independence and to say good-bye to childish things, which means accepting the responsibilities of adulthood.

Garbage

indicates that it is time for the dreamer to give life a good spring clean. Memories of experiences that have been holding us back should be discarded so that we can move on. Those from which we can learn should be taken off the shelf, dusted down and re-examined for the potential they still hold. Garbage, especially if it is the sort of kitchen debris that older readers may recall as being set aside for pig swill, can be the body's (and the brain is a part of the body) way of telling us that we should take time out to make sure that we are doing everything we can to maintain our health. To dream that you are collecting garbage can say that you are starting to doubt some of the assumptions on which you have founded your life – especially your moral code. And if you dream that you are disposing of garbage, then you may be concerned that you will be asked to defend someone whose reputation has become tainted by the mess he is making of his life.

Gas

has among its meanings one very sensible one. If you dream that you smell gas, then the chances are that it is not a dream, but that your 'sleeping' brain is registering that you are actually smelling gas and is warning you to wake up! Even if the merest whiff is smelt, then first thing on waking have all your appliances checked. Otherwise, its appearance in dreams is an indication that we are having difficulties in controlling many aspects of our lives that we should be able to reign in – our thoughts, feelings and how we use our abilities mainly. Gas can also be an acknowledgement of the power of the Spirit, something to which the dreamer has probably given little attention of late. Smelling gas and searching for its source can suggest that friends are displeased with you for some reason. Deep down, you know what and the dream tells you that it is up to you to make amends. And if the dream concerns cooking with gas, then you can look forward to waving adversity goodbye and giving the fruits of success a warm welcome.

Glass

represents the invisible barrier that we put between ourselves and the rest of the world to keep it at bay. It's something we all do, no matter how gregarious we see ourselves as being. And just as glass represents our barriers, it also represents other people's. Or as one cynic put it, glass says that we all know that self-defence is the best form of attack. If the glass is of the frosted or smoked variety then the dreamer has a 'DO NOT DISTURB' sign deeply engraved on his or her emotions. To dream that we are breaking glass is an expression of our awareness that if we all took down our barriers, then maybe, just maybe, we would all be better off for it. Trapped emotions could be set free and we could all relax and move on. Glass that has already been broken predicts that life is about to change – for the better if the glass is sparkling, for the worse if it's cloudy. If dreamers see themselves drinking out of gleamingly clean glasses, they are about to sip from the cup of good fortune.

Gongs

being rung in our dreams announce either that a target set has now been reached, or if not reached we have gone as far as we can go towards achieving it and now must seek the approval of others before going any further. To see ourselves as striking a gong indicates our need for extra strength to see us through the immediate future. Such strength may be physical but is much more likely to be emotional. Gongs can also serve as an alarm call to wake us up to the fact that we have been neglecting the spiritual side of life and that if we are to be seen by our peers as well-rounded people, we need to pay it significant attention.

Guillotines

feature more in the dreams of those who live in countries where they were once used as a means of capital punishment. But we are all aware of what they are, and although not common they do appear in our dreams. When they do, they may indicate a fear of lack of self-control or loss of dignity, or a dislike of anything to which we cannot give a logical explanation when it enters our lives. They can indicate an awareness of the potential to cut ourselves off from those we love, or indeed that we have lost the capacity to love altogether. To paraphrase the hero of Charles Dickens' A Tale of Two Cities – there are far, far better dreams to dream – but there are far, far worse ones, too.

Haggard

faces in a dream are two warnings in one! First, they have been noted many times as having appeared in the dreams of those who a little later wake up to realize that their love life is

69

heading for disaster and there is nothing they can do about it, for when the realization sets in, it's too late. And there are almost as many instances of such faces being seen by dreamers who later find that their businesses are in a precarious state of affairs. If it's your own face that appears lined, worried and aged, then keep a look out over your shoulder for ill health. If the dream is accompanied by a feeling of being tired, that's a warning to slow down, you're going too fast.

Hair

has about as many meanings as there are hairs on the human head! For a woman to dream that she is combing a head of thick, lustrous hair warns her that she will neglect her personal affairs and that in doing so her career will suffer. Men who dream that they are going bald or that their hair is thinning are being warned that their generosity will cost them dear and that some sort of psychological illness might be threatening. If a woman dreams that she is losing her hair, the dream tells her that she will have to work hard to earn her living. Hair that is turning grey presages illness in the family or in the circle of closest friends. Snowy white hair, on the other hand, presages a life full of fortune. Hair that is dreamed of by men as turning pure white overnight while the face stays young and unlined warns of extremely bad news coming soon. For a woman to have such a dream is a warning that a sudden illness or accident will rob her of her lover. For a man to dream that he has thick, black curly hair tells that although he is seen as hugely charming by women, they don't trust him. And for a woman to dream that she has similar hair suggests that someone she trusts implicitly might be about to try to seduce her. Male dreamers who see a woman with shining gold hair are being told that women see them as true friends and fearless lovers. Red hair in general suggests change is on the horizon. And for a man to dream that his lover has red hair tells him that she is being or will be unfaithful. Brown hair is bad news for dreamers who are considering a first career or a change of job: the choice they make is likely to be the wrong one.

Handcuffs

are a strong indication that the dreamer fears he is being restrained in some way. The restraint may be put in our paths by someone who holds authority over us, or it may be our own doubts and fears that are holding us back, restraining us from reaching our true potential. A dreamer who dreams that he is putting handcuffs on someone he recognizes is acknowledging a desire to bind that person to him and that deep down there is a possessiveness in his feelings towards the person who is being handcuffed.

Hands

are the parts of our bodies that we all use, often unknowingly, when we express ourselves, and they express themselves significantly in the sign language that is dreams. If they are seen holding different objects, then some sort of conflict is presaged, probably between what the dreamer believes in and what he feels. If a hand is seen clamped across the breast, then the dreamer is about to submit in a situation that has long been bothersome. If the hands are clasped, a new friendship is indicated or perhaps an existing one is about to deepen into something special. A hand clenched into a fist warns the dreamer of a looming threat. If the hands are folded, then the dreamer is being told that it is time to relax and rest more. Hands covering the eyes suggest that the dreamer has done something about which he is deeply ashamed or even horrified. Someone who feels that restrictions of some sort are in place may well dream of a pair of hands crossed at the wrists. If a hand is

71

offered to another person, then the dreamer is acknowledging that surrender may be the only way to unblock the path ahead. If the palms of the hands are facing outwards, then the dreamer is being told to give the blessing for which he has been asked. But if the hands are pressing on either side of the head, then the dreamer is being advised to think long and hard before taking the course of action to which he is being pressed. Washing the hands in a dream is a sign that the dreamer considers himself innocent of some charge that has been levied against him.

Halters

suggest that the dreamer has been keeping too tight a rein on his intellect, and that if only he could find the courage to loosen it, he would gallop ahead, especially in creative matters. Even those who are about as creative as a dead sheep should think what such a creature becomes in the hands of artist Damien Hirst, and they could be surprised at what they might achieve if they take the dream as a suggestion to try to be a little more imaginative. To dream of putting a halter on a horse denotes that the dreamer is looking for someone to show him the way to a life of deeper spiritual satisfaction. And in gypsy tradition, to see a young horse being put to the halter for the first time is to be told that a recently made acquaintance will put a business proposition the dreamer's way, and the dreamer would do well to consider it seriously.

Harems

are the stuff of which many male dreams are made, and they may make the male dreamer seem macho when he sees himself strutting among his concubines. In fact analysts believe that such a dream is a sign that he is aware he has a feminine side but that he is struggling to come to terms with its complexities.

For female dreamers to see themselves in a harem indicates that they are totally at ease with their sensual nature, indeed enjoy it considerably. Such a dream can also suggest that the dreamer feels a need for the companionship of other women, perhaps to be part of a sorority with the members of which she can share problems and common experiences. More romantic interpretations say that the dreamer is being warned that he is wasting his energies in the pursuit of belittling pleasures. But the leopard can change its spots and if the energies are properly channelled then the dreamer's true promise and potential can, and will, be realized. On the same level, if a woman dreams such a dream, she may be tempted to indulge in adultery. If she sees herself as favourite concubine she will be offered the chance to indulge in material pleasures – but the opportunity will soon be whisked away from her and she will come down to Earth with a bang.

Hieroglyphics

the meaning of these was lost to us from Ancient Egyptian times until the early nineteenth-century when the symbols were successfully interpreted. They foretell of hardships experienced while deciding which career path to follow. But if you dream that you can read these strange pictograms and understand what they say, then the obstacles that will be put in your path will be temporary and easily overcome on your way to considerable success.

Historical

settings indicate that the dreamer feels the need to get in touch with his or her past in order to come to terms with something that is clouding the sunshine today. Some interpreters believe that the earlier the setting, the farther back the dreamer has to go to get to the root of the problem, but that may be putting too literal an interpretation on things. The dream can also be a sign that the dreamer looks on the way things were with fond nostalgia and wishes that the clock could be turned back.

Hooks

tell the dreamer that deep inside him he has the power to draw things to him, and that it is up to him whether to use this ability for the general good or otherwise. Or, to see a hook can indicate that the dreamer feels he has been unfairly lured to do something that would normally have gone against his nature or instincts, and that in being so hooked he is afraid that his freedom has been severely restricted. Travelling folk believe that to dream of a hook means to be burdened by unhappy duties.

Hospitals

are good news for the dreamer, not so good for those he or she knows! When dreamers see themselves as being patients in hospital, then there may well be an epidemic of some sort about to sweep the country. The dreamer will not be affected by it: the people he or she knows will not be so lucky. For people to dream that they are visiting friends or relatives in hospitals is an indication that sad news about an absent friend will soon be heard. To be seen leaving a hospital, having been confined there, suggests that the dreamer will be worried by the escapades of enemies, but that he or she will gain the upper hand and send them packing, licking their wounds.

Houses

are almost always a reference to the soul and that which attempts to give structure to our spiritual and corporeal lives. If the dream house is shared with another person, then the dreamer may be feeling threatened by an aspect of his personality that he has long kept hidden but that is threatening to make itself public. If different parts of the house are being used for different purposes, then the dreamer is becoming increasingly aware of an inner conflict between two aspects of his personality that is making him feel uneasy. The front of the house is thought by interpreters to represent the face that we present to the world. Entering or leaving the house is, it is thought, the psyche's way of telling the dreamer that a certain situation should be faced in an introvert or extrovert fashion respectively.

Hurricanes

have various meanings – none of them good! To hear or see one heading your way suggests that you are going to have your work cut out to survive a downturn in business. To be in a house that is being buffeted by hurricane-force winds indicates you may have to flee to far-off places to avoid some sort of business or emotional disaster. And it may be that no matter how far you go, your past will forever be snapping at your heels. If you see yourself looking at the aftermath of a terrible hurricane, you will sail close to the winds of disaster but a white knight will ride to your rescue at the very last minute. To see dead bodies being dragged from the havoc caused by a hurricane says that the troubles of another, probably a family member, will cause you great distress. To dream of a hurricane can serve as a warning that you will be dragged into a legal dispute in which you have no real involvement but that both parties will try to get you on their side. Best to stay neutral and avoid the recriminations that are certain to follow if you do get involved.

Ice

can say that the dreamer sees himself as being something of a cold fish – and unless he can be seen to be warmer in relationships with family and any friends that he may have made, they may give up on him. It can also indicate a failure to grasp the significance of what is happening all around and that this inability is creating an impression of being hopelessly out of touch. On a more ethereal level, ice can be seen as a sign that the dreamer has frozen out something concerning the past and that before he or she can move on, whatever it is has to be taken out of the freezer and put in the defrost compartment. Dark, dirty ice, gypsies believe, augurs that bad feeling between friends could cause problems, or worse that you have innocently done something that has caused those who were previously indifferent to become filled with jealousy to such an extent that they are out to get you at any cost. To unmarried women, blocks of clear ice could presage becoming engaged in the near future. (This is an American interpretation and is likely to have come about because of the use of the word 'ice' as slang for diamonds.)

Icicles

when they hang from a wall, according to Shakespeare in Love's Labour's Lost, icicles herald the owl's merry note. But to the dreamer, they suggest a feeling that support from those who might be expected to provide it has been sadly lacking of late and that this has had a detrimental effect on things, particularly at work. To see them melting drip by drip says that troubles will likewise start to melt. And if they are seen to do this on the roof of the house means, according to Romany tradition, that marital troubles will end to be replaced by a long period of domestic harmony. The same tradition holds that to see them melting from trees suggests trouble of some sort concerning property. To see them forming is a sign of troubles creeping up and catching the dreamer unawares, but also that something equally unexpected will give him the ammunition to see them off.

Imitation

can be seen as a sign that the dreamer is certain that the course of action that has been followed regarding a recent circumstance was the correct one, and that family, friends and colleagues alike should all show some sign of gratitude. Being imitated in a dream can also suggest that the dreamer feels lacking in leadership skills despite being assured by others that he has them in spades. To see ourselves imitating one of our peers in a flattering fashion suggests that we have the conceit to believe that we could do just as good a job as they are doing regardless of the heights they have scaled. However, if the person we are imitating is superior to us intellectually, then the dream is an acknowledgement that they have a deeper knowledge and understanding of things than we have – although that might change if we apply ourselves. If the imitation is intentionally unflattering then deep down we may be feeling that our behaviour of late has been lacking in integrity. Dream interpreters of times gone by believed that dreams featuring imitation served as a warning against being palmed off with something that would become a source of trouble. And if a girl dreamed that someone was imitating her lover, then the word 'fidelity' was one with which he was probably unfamiliar.

Infidelity

whether it is being seen as practised by dreamer or partner, infidelity serves as a warning to be more circumspect about your actions not just with each other but with the opposite sex in general. If the warning goes unheeded, the consequences could be considerable. To dream of being unfaithful with more than one other person is a sign of a guilty conscience about something, though this does not necessarily relate to affairs of the heart.

Inventors

are regarded as linking us with the more creative side of our nature, not in the artistic sense perhaps, but more likely that part that we all have that enables us to grasp an idea and give it practical vent. To see one in a dream suggests that the dreamer is slowly realizing this and is willing to be more flexible and receptive to new ideas. Another, perhaps more fanciful, meaning handed down from generation to generation is that to dream of an inventor is to be told that an honour in recognition of a unique achievement will be bestowed on the dreamer. And to dream of actually inventing something denotes that aspirations to wealth and good fortune will be realized and that success will follow the dreamer in whichever direction he wishes to travel.

Jars

are seen as being concerned with the feminine and the maternal and are a sign that the dreamer is coming round to acknowledge the debt owed to both of these qualities. It may be that holding back this recognition has prevented the dreamer developing into a complete person, and that this may now happen. Another interpretation is that when they are full jars are synonymous with success and victory, but dreamed of as being empty they denote heartbreak and illness. A curious American interpretation is that to dream of foods usually sold in cans as being seen in jars is to be told that if frugality is practised for the time being, and that if any financial surpluses are saved rather than spent, the dividends they will yield will grow into significant sums. To dream of ourselves being jarred or shaken is an indication that while we may be moving forward in life, we are not firmly in the driver's seat and are consequently being put in a position where we are at risk of being hurt or knocked off our chosen path.

Jealousy

of another's good fortune augurs that the dreamer's path to the top will be a risky affair and if the top job is achieved, then it will be an uncomfortable tenure as others will be constantly plotting to usurp the chairman's seat on the board. To be jealous of a spouse is to be warned that if enemies are not already plotting against you, they soon will be. If the dreamer is a young woman and she dreams that she is jealous of her lover, then a gypsy seer would tell her that her swain's eyes are already wandering in another's direction.

Jubilees

hold special significance for dreamers who believe that life goes in seven-year cycles. This makes the fiftieth year especially significant, being the first year after the completion of seven such cycles. Dreams associated with such a celebration are thought, therefore, to indicate the successful completion of a rite of passage and the dawn of a new age. They also denote that the dreamer will be a participant in many pleasurable enterprises, especially if the dreamer is a young woman and the pleasurable enterprise she has on her mind is marriage. To dream of a religious jubilee was, according to Romany people, a sign that the dreamers would never travel far from home, and their lives would be unmarked by great unhappiness.

Juries

suggest that the dreamer is keen to gain the approval of his peers and is afraid that he may struggle to achieve it, because they will fail to appreciate the motives that caused a certain choice to be made. If the dreamer sees himself being acquitted by twelve good men and true, then business is set to run smoothly. But if the verdict is 'Guilty!' he will be harassed by enemies to the point that his endurance will be tested to the limit. To see oneself as sitting on a jury was, according to tradition, a sign that job dissatisfaction was brewing and that it was time to explore new horizons on the career front. If we disagree with our fellow jurors, then we may be on the point of kissing convention goodbye and going our own way. And if we're in the majority, then we are happy with the course our life is taking.

Kaleidoscopes

are an indication that the dreamer enjoyed the freedom that childhood offered while at the same time appreciating the disciplines that parents imposed. To dream of one in adulthood may be an acknowledgement that the dreamer has been indulging in too much freedom and that he would like someone to tell him to put the brakes on. They can also indicate an awareness that there is a reservoir of creative ability that is, as yet, untapped. And just as the designs that are seen through a kaleidoscope change every time the wheel is turned, so the dreamer feels a sense of awe every time the wheel of life turns and circumstances constantly change. But to dream of these constantly changing designs could mean that young dreamers are having a hard time making up their minds what to do with their lives. If the wheel settles on a particularly pleasing design, then not only will the dreamer make the right choice in career, their choice of lover will be the right one. But if the pattern is ugly and distorted, the future may hold more disappointments than can normally be expected.

Keys

open the door to fresh opportunities. They do this by telling us to unlock memories that have been pushed to the far corners of our minds and to make us remember experiences and lessons that we had long forgotten. And they say that if we heed what they tell us then we will find the answers to many puzzling questions about how we have come to where we are in life. Most exciting of all, they tell us that if we use them, it's not too late to learn and to live a much more rewarding life. To see yourself finding another's keys is to be told that domestic happiness is yours for the asking. If we see ourselves as having lost them, then an unpleasant adventure of some sort is just around the corner. To see broken keys is to be told that married life will be marked by quarrels and long separations. And to give away keys in a dream is to be warned that poor judgement will lead to making many errors that could easily have been avoided.

Kisses

of a gentle, loving nature being given to or by someone we love are generally an omen of good that shows that the dreamer is at peace and happy with himself. But if the kiss is unwelcome the dreamer may awake to find that the immediate future is marred by myriad tiny vexations. Kissing someone we have known for some time may be a sign that something was holding us back from seeing them as true friends but whatever it was has now been removed and we finally accept the person for what they are. It can also suggest that the person we are kissing possesses a quality that we would like to have ourselves. Traditionally, Romany people believed that to kiss children meant a happy family reunion and contentment in work, while kissing your mother was an indication of success and honours to come. To kiss an enemy presaged reconciliation, while to kiss a stranger suggested that the dreamer was possessed of a louche nature. The list is almost endless – with different interpretations being put on who was being kissed and where the kiss was aimed! But perhaps the Romany interpretation could be summed up as to dream of enjoying a kiss properly bestowed on a person with whom one is properly acquainted is good news. Anything else usually spells trouble.

Kites

recall the happy, carefree, irresponsible days of childhood. To dream of them is to acknowledge a need for spiritual freedom. They can also suggest that deep down the dreamer sees himself as something of a popinjay – and that there is a fear that some-one will see through the bluster and reveal to all the shallow creature that lies beneath the façade. To dream of making a kite suggests that the dreamer will speculate a little in the hope of making a lot – and that all the 'littles' will soon start to mount to the gambler's disadvantage.

Knots

a common interpretation is that the simpler the knot, the greater the urgency to take a new direction in seeking the solu-tion to a problem. And the more complicated it is, then the stronger the dreamer's feeling that it is only a sense of duty or even guilt that is keeping him or her bound to a certain situation. The way out of it is to loosen the ties, but the dream suggests a reluctance to do so. On a superficial level knots sug-gest that what appear to be trifling affairs are going to cause dis-proportionate problems: and to dream of tying a knot is indica-tive of the dreamer's independent nature and a stubborn refusal to give in to the nagging of an equally obstinate spouse or friend. Knots can suggest that the dreamer is facing what is seen as an insoluble problem. The dream is the subconscious's way of suggesting that a gradual approach is better than the one taken by Alexander the Great who, when faced with the Gordian knot, unsheathed his sword and sliced through it!

Labels

are associated with the deeply felt need that lies within all of us (despite appearances) to conform to society's mores. From birth, we are labelled with the names our parents give us, and when we dream of labels we are identifying with the need to name things, for without names and labels life wouldn't make sense. And so, to dream of labels is to acknowledge the search for order in your life. To dream of something being incorrectly labelled suggests awareness that we have failed to understand something correctly. Correspondingly, to dream of relabelling something is the subconscious's way of telling us that we have to put this right. To dream of reading a label suggests that you have let someone know your personal business or revealed your true feelings to them and this may have caused them considerable unhappiness.

Laboratories

can indicate that the dreamer has an unexpressed desire to approach life in a more logical and scientific way and in so doing wants to develop unexploited talents and abilities. The same dream might suggest an awareness that the dreamer is frittering time and energies in business ventures that are mediocre. If the dream concerns an experiment that fails, the dreamer's business may well follow suit. But if the experiment succeeds, then so too will career matters. If a breakthrough is seen to be made, a new idea will lead to brilliant success.

Lacing up shoes

is believed by many to be symbolic of death – not necessarily a physical death but perhaps a farewell to someone whom the dreamer has known for a long time and whose friendship and wisdom he values.

Ladders

often feature in the dreams of those who are in the throes of changing jobs. Hardly surprising when one thinks of the connections between the two – the dreamer is climbing the career ladder, ladders are used to move from one location to another and the dreamer is doing likewise. In this context they confirm that the dreamer believes that he is making the right move at the right time – as long as he is carrying the ladder and it is in perfect condition. If the rungs are broken, the transition may be difficult, and if someone else has the ladder, then the progress may depend on the help of colleagues. Ladders can also acknowledge that the time is right to make a move towards a more spiritual life. Interpretations from days gone by include that to see oneself falling from a ladder is a sign that present endeavours will be unsuccessful, and that if someone is steadying a ladder up which the dreamer is climbing, then the heights of the career ladder will be easily achieved.

Languages

heard but not understood are a sign that we are aware that something is not right in our lives, but we are not quite sure what. They can also indicate a desire to let various aspects of our personalities play a more positive part in our lives – in other words, to speak for themselves. They may suggest that the dreamer is having difficulties understanding the motives behind the actions of a friend. In the days when classics were more widely taught in schools, Latin was thought to herald a victory or a distinction of some kind, while to dream of Greek suggested that the dreamer's ideas would be widely discussed and eventually accepted. Foul language is a sign that the dreamer will find him or herself at the centre of an embarrassing situation brought about by another person's thoughtless actions.

Lawyers

dreaming of lawyers is said to indicate that bad news or a loss, perhaps both, may soon strike. If the dreamer is about to enter into a contract or embark on a new business venture, the appearance of a man of the law should be taken as a clear warning to carry out some more homework before signing on the dotted line.

Lead

points to disappointment in many directions. For a man, to dream of a lead mine warns that the docile girl he marries will turn out to be a deceitful shrew, and that business ventures will be viewed with suspicion by friends and colleagues alike. And to dream of molten lead forewarns that impatience will lead you and your friends down the path of failure.

Leaves

green leaves presage growth, which equals good health, prosperity and a prospective vigorous love life. Brown leaves, perhaps walking through a carpet of them, mean just the opposite. Walking through a rain of falling leaves can be positive as it suggests that you should stop wasting parts of your life, personal or business.

Lemons

feature in dreams that are often as sharp as the fruits themselves. A healthy lemon tree with lots of fruits and rich foliage equals jealousy, usually misplaced. Eating lemons suggests eating one's words, or some other humiliation. In Middle Eastern culture to dream of dried lemons (not a common dream) means divorce or separation. Green lemons, not that common north of the Mediterranean, also bode ill.

Lentils

are not commonly dreamt about in northern countries, but are becoming more evident as they appear on international menus. They don't suggest anything good anyway. As they are dried,

they often suggest barren relationships and unhealthy surroundings. But within their dried exterior there is goodness
which can suggest that a difficult relationship might be worth
sticking with. Things may turn out all right.

Leopards

those most elegant of big cats forewarn that misplaced confidence may endanger plans that seem set for success. But if the
dreamer slays the beast, victory is his or hers in any dispute. A
leopard padding to and fro in a cage says that the dreamer is
surrounded by enemies but that they will be seen off.

Lettuce

dreamed about in any of its many varieties has been recorded
over the years as being connected with embarrassment which
turns out well, providing you see it growing. Eating it is a different matter. It can engender jealousy and envy. The green
connection? Sowing lettuce, first reported in the early 1900s,
and not a common activity, denotes early sickness and death.
Dreams of buying lettuce suggest you will be the architect of
your own downfall.

Libraries

being the rooms (albeit it in grander houses) where books and
by implication knowledge are stored, libraries are often taken as
being symbolic of our minds and how we store and cope with
the information we receive.

Lightning

that strikes an object close to the dreamer causing them to feel
the shock is a warning that your name is on the tongues of malicious gossipmongers. It also means that good fortune about to
hit a friend will have an adverse affect on the dreamer. To be

struck by lightning means that something terrible is about to happen in business or love affairs. But if the lightning flashes above the dreamer's head, happiness and a windfall of some sort are coming the dreamer's way.

Lilies

elegant symbols of purity and innocence, lilies suggest that happiness will soon bloom in the dreamer's life and that it will be achieved through virtue. To dream of lily of the valley tells the dreamer that to achieve happiness, he or she should act with humility. Water lilies foretell that regeneration in some form is in the offing. Lotus lilies herald a new birth and a long life, while tiger lilies warn the dreamer that temptation of some sort, probably wealth, will be put in his path.

Limbs

in general suggest that the dreamer is having doubts about his or her sexuality. If an arm or a leg is being pulled from the torso, then these doubts are literally tearing them apart, and threatening them to the very roots of their existence. If sexuality is not the issue, and arms and legs are seen repeatedly, then we are being told to dismantle our lives and start again.

Limping

is a warning that something you have been looking forward to for some time will be marred by an unexpected worry. To dream that someone else is limping tells you that a friend will do something in all innocence that will cause you great offence.

Linen clothes

are comfortable to wear and good to dream of, unless soiled. Fresh, clean linen says that good news is about to come your way, and that your current love is the one you will spend the rest of your life with in complete harmony. But if the linen is grubby, poverty may be about to rear its unwelcome head, love might be about to evaporate from a relationship and if that wasn't enough, then something you treasure could go missing.

Lions

king of all they survey, lions empower the dreamer with a driving force that will take him or her by surprise. Surviving an attack by a lion heralds victory in any conflict: being defeated by one forewarns that an enemy's attack will be successful. A lion baring its teeth threatens those seeking more power, especially in their careers, with defeat. But a dream filled with a lion's roar tells a male dreamer that he will find favour with the opposite sex.

Lips

that are full and luscious and red say to the dreamer that good times are just around the corner – if they have not already shown themselves. Relationships will hum harmoniously and there are affluent times ahead. If the dreamer is in love, then lips such as these indicate that the love will be reciprocated. Swollen lips, on the other hand, speak of sour marital relations, ill-tempered meetings and being forced to make decisions that will turn out to be the wrong ones. Thin lips whisper to the dreamer that he will be able to master the details of any subject to which he turns his mind.

Looking for a job

in a dream is quite straightforward for once. Being unable to find one is indicative that you are loyal to your present employer and have no intention of making a move. Finding one, on the other hand, suggests that you may find yourself knocking on prospective employers' doors in the very near future.

Losing luggage

is a common dream (and who among us has not in real life stood by a baggage carousel at an airport, quite convinced that our luggage will never appear?). In dreams it denotes that a recent investment might prove to be unwise. This is not necessarily a financial investment: it could be that we invested time unwisely, or our emotions. The outcome could be distress in the family, particularly if it is the latter case. If a single person dreams of losing his or her luggage, then a broken engagement is foretold.

Lotteries

indicate that the dreamer may be possessed of a lazy nature, especially in his job, where he expects to be well paid in return for very little effort. They can also suggest that he is the kind of person who is prepared to take a risk if he can see that the gain might far outweigh the input. Another interpretation of dreaming of lotteries is that carelessness could lead to disappointment. If the dream concerns losing a lottery, then beware lest false friends cause you to become the victim of circumstances. The news is not better if you dream of winning the lottery, for in that case something unpleasant is on the cards. But if you dream that someone else has won, then fun times with friends lie ahead.

Luggage

portends that the dreamer will soon be weighed down with burdensome and unpleasant duties, probably involving people whom the dreamer finds unsavoury. To see oneself carrying one's own luggage while porters are standing around doing nothing suggests that something so distressing is about to happen that it will preoccupy the dreamer to such an extent that he will be blind to the concerns of others.

Lungs

may warn that clouds of grief are forming on the horizon and are about to blow in to darken the dreamer's life. Alternatively, they may flag the fact that very important decisions can be put off no longer and have to be made right away.

Macaroni

seen in large quantities tells the dreamer that if strict economies are made in any direction, the dividend will far outweigh the sacrifice made. But to dream of eating it warns that losses may hit the dreamer's pocket – not large, but a loss is a loss! If the dreamer is a young woman and she sees uncooked macaroni, then she can expect a stranger to enter her life and influence it in an unexpected way.

Machines

may indicate a concern with the body's functions: indeed it has been noted that people struck down by illnesses that are usually not diagnosed until they are fairly well advanced report that machines featured in their dreams some time before any physical symptoms appeared. Dream machines are also seen as representing logical thinking. If they are seen as being in perfect working order, then the dreamer is likely to be the sort of person others turn to for advice to see them through a difficult situation. Well-oiled, smooth-running machinery is seen as a sign that the dreamer is more than happy with domestic matters, but to dream of being caught or injured in a machine is a warning that unhappiness and loss loom large on the horizon.

Maggots

are generally thought to be an indication that the dreamer is concerned about death – not a physically imminent one, but the spiritual aspect of passing from one stage of being to another.

They can also suggest that the dreamer feels that there is something within him – an idea, a feeling perhaps – that should not be there, and that is making him feel impure in some way. Their appearance has also been seen as a warning that a lazy acquaintance has been subtly leeching on the dreamer who is only now becoming aware that he is being used.

Mansions

and good fortune go hand in hand and to dream of being in one suggests that the dreamer will never go hungry and will never know the feeling that there is too much month at the end of a salary cheque! To see a mansion in the distance portends that the good life beckons but not in the immediate future. There is one curious exception to the good fortune that mansions herald: if someone dreams of being in a haunted mansion, then some unexpected misfortune will shatter the dreamer's present contentment.

Marble

is a cold stone and to dream of a marble quarry tells that the dreamer may be warmed by financial success, but his life will be a chill one, devoid of any affection whatsoever. If the marble is being polished, an inheritance, not necessarily of a financial nature, but pleasing nonetheless, will soon be revealed. To dream of dropping a piece of marble and seeing it smash into pieces is a sign that disfavour brought on by a lapse of morals will soon cloud the dreamer's life.

Marigolds

symbolize that a new love will prove to be long-lasting and constant. A marriage in the offing will be long and happy. And if that isn't enough this generous flower promises advancement in career matters and rich rewards coming the dreamer's way.

Marmalade

is said to have been given its name by the chef to Mary, Queen of Scots while she was married to the dauphin of France. When the young princess fell ill, the young chef concocted a jelly of quinces and herbs for 'Marie malade' and the two words became corrupted to the one we know today. Maybe that is why to dream of marmalade warns that a bout of ill health is on the cards.

Masons

suggest that you are about to carve yourself opportunities that will gain you promotion at work and a consequent rise in social status. If the masons are the sort who belong to the Masonic Order and they are wearing their aprons and regalia of office, then they serve to remind you that you have a responsibility towards others who look to you to protect them from the evils of life.

Meals

in general suggest that the dreamer is paying too much attention to too much detail in business matters and that this is stopping him seeing the overall picture.

Measles

say that it's time to relax, for if you become over-anxious, particularly about business affairs, your health could suffer.

Meat

if cooked, and dreamed of by a woman, meat warns her that what she is working towards will be snatched from her and given to another. If the meat is uncooked, then she will achieve her goal, but only after she has overcome discouragement from many directions. For dreamers of either sex, roast meat is a sign that a spouse, if not already being unfaithful, may be on the verge of being so. If the dreamer is carving a joint of meat, then an investment recently made will have been ill-judged. But it's not too late to withdraw and look elsewhere.

Mechanics

herald a change of address and an upturn in business if the dreamer is self-employed. If he or she is employed in a business that has been struggling to survive, the appearance of a mechanic in a dream can suggest that business is about to pick up and then boom to such an extent that there may soon be more in the salary cheque within a month or two.

Medicine

the meaning depends on the medicine's taste! If it is sweet then there's trouble in store, but the dreamer will survive and grow in stature as a result. If on the other hand, the medicine tastes foul, then serious illness threatens, or if it doesn't materialize the alternative is just as worrying – sorrow and loss, deep sorrow and significant loss. For a dreamer to administer medicine is a sign that someone who trusts you is about to be disappointed in you.

Memorials

can serve as recognition that the dreamer feels a deep-rooted but unspoken, perhaps unacknowledged, nostalgia for a time in life which was much happier than at present. They are also, perhaps, the subconscious's way of taking the reader back to an unpleasant memory that is indelibly imprinted on the dreamer's mind. If this is the case, the dreamer is being told to come to terms with it and to leave it behind if it is not to surface as a ball and chain that will prevent full potential being realized. Romanies believed that to dream of a memorial signified that the dreamer would soon be called upon to be particularly kind to relations who were threatened with sickness or financial difficulty.

Men

if they are tall, dark and handsome, men tell the dreamer that enjoyable times are round the corner, and that if they are already here, then they will get even better. But if the dream male is not blessed in the looks department, then instead of good times read disappointment! If the dreamer is female, a male in a dream signifies that she should look to her masculine side and if she does this she will increase her chances of success in business. If her dream man is indeed a dream man, then she will find herself being offered a distinction of some sort, maybe in her career or maybe as recognition of charity work. If, on the other hand, he is ugly, someone she thinks of as a friend will bring her trouble in some shape or form. An older man is thought to represent the innate wisdom that lies deep within us all.

Mercury

indicates that someone is plotting against you and could cause you to have to make unhappy changes in your life. Featuring in female dreams, it warns that separation from her family, perhaps brought about by desertion, is about to bring the dreamer unhappiness.

Milk

has a variety of meanings for the dreamer. Farmers can expect a good harvest and travellers safe passage. To dream that one is giving milk away warns that overgenerosity may cause problems in financial matters. Spilt milk warns that the actions of a friend will cause you short-lived unhappiness brought about by a loss of some kind. To dream of milk that has gone off is prescient of lots of niggling problems coming up – nothing serious but distracting nonetheless. Reaching for a glass of milk that stays Tantalus-style, just out of reach, signifies that a valued friendship is about to come to an end abruptly or that something of value will be lost. To dream of hot milk promises that ambitions will be realized but only after some hard-fought battles have had to be won. And lastly, to dream of bathing Cleopatra-like in milk indicates that the companionship of good friends will soon warm your life.

Minerals

of an unspecified nature suggest that difficulties that are at present being experienced will shortly be overcome and that sunshine is about to peek through the clouds that have been darkening the horizon. However, if the dream concerns walking over land that is being mined, then beware, for there is distress in the offing. It will pass, though, but it will have a lasting effect upon your life.

Missing a train

was considered by Freud to indicate a fear of death, a feeling of sexual inadequacy or of being incapable of coping with some relationship or other. Havelock Ellis takes a much more prosaic view. According to his writing, missing a train indicated that the dreamer had a headache! Others agree – almost, believing as they do that the underlying cause is physical or mental exhaustion. Some interpreters see the dream as suggesting a regret of missed opportunities or an acknowledgement that the dreamer is unable to cope with life as it is now. A more imaginative interpretation is that missing a train indicates that a move of house or a long journey is likely or that a friend from far away is about to visit.

Mistletoe

sacred to Pagans, Druids and followers of New Age ways of life, and under sprigs of which revellers kiss at Christmas, blesses dreamers with good fortune and promises of ongoing good health.

Money

is linked to the value the dreamer puts on himself. To see it suggests that he is starting to question that value because there may be a deep-rooted suspicion that he may be selling himself short. To dream of finding money is seen by many as a sign that the dreamer will experience many small worries but that on balance a happy life will be enjoyed. To see oneself paying out cash is a sign that misfortune may be on the way. If you see yourself counting money and finding yourself short, then if the bills are not already piling up on your desk, it is just a matter of time before they do. It is even worse to see yourself stealing money, for then your finances are in real danger of collapsing.

Monkeys

warn that fawning friends will flatter to get their own way at the dreamer's expense. A young woman who dreams of feeding a monkey will be betrayed by such flattering. But if the monkey is dead, then enemies will cease to feature in your life.

Monks

bring family quarrels in their wake, and may be news that some sort of unpleasant journey may have to be made. To dream that one is a monk suggests that a loss of some kind is imminent. If it is a female whose dreams a monk enters, she may be about to find herself the target of some particularly malicious gossip.

The Moon

has, since time immemorial, been seen as representative of the feminine and emotional side of the psyche – which is why it is often referred to as Lady Moon. When she lights up your dreams, she is telling men and women alike that the time is ripe to listen to what the feminine side is saying and to pay more attention to emotional thinking than cool logic. It may be that male dreamers who see the Moon are, deep down, afraid of women: the dream tells them not to be. To the female dreamer, the Moon suggests that she should draw strength from the sorority of other women. According to gypsies, to see the Moon in an exceptionally starry sky is a sign of great material success, but to see it in anything other than full glory is a sign that disappointment is on the cards, especially where the behaviour of a spouse is concerned.

Moss

clings to the rocks on which it spreads, and if it features in a dream it suggests that wealth will spread in the dreamer's direction and that it will cling to him or her.

Mothers

are the people with whom we forge our first significant relationships, so it is not surprising that they feature so often in dreams. If your mother appears in your dream as she is in real life, then she is giving her blessing to any enterprises you are involved with and they should turn out well. If you are talking to her, then you will soon receive good news about a business that has been concerning you. For a woman to dream of her mother tells her that her marriage will be happy and that her life will be full of pleasant duties. If the dreamer sees his or her mother as emaciated or worse, dead, then huge sadness will follow, while to hear her cry out as if in pain is almost as bad – for there is menace in the air. To hear her call out warns that business colleagues think you have been making bad decisions or that you have been derelict in carrying out your duties. And being such important figures in our lives, there is more about mothers. If a man sees his mother being transformed into another woman he is being told that it's time to let his mother go: that other women are just as important, if not at present then perhaps later.

Mothers-in-law

say that there's going to be a serious disagreement some time soon but that peaceful relations will soon be restored and the reconciliation will find the relationship, be it a family one or a friendship, is strengthened as a result.

Mountaineering

not unexpectedly suggests that ambitions are yet to be realized and that the closer the dreamer sees himself to the summit, then the closer to achieving his ambitions he is. Often the dreamer sees himself as being almost there but realizes that the last step is the most difficult to take. But hold on – the summit is there to be scaled. And if he has reached the peak, then that's it. At best, the dreamer is on a plateau as far as career matters are concerned: at worst, it's all downhill from now onwards!

Moving house

tells that the dreamer has an as yet unspoken desire for change. If the house is a larger one than the one at present lived in, that's indicative of a desire to live a more open life. If the house is smaller, then the dreamer may be feeling a need to unburden himself or herself of something that has been gnawing away at him or her for some time.

Murder

generally suggests that the dreamer is struggling to control some part of his nature or an instinct that he does not trust. If he is the victim then it signifies that his life is way out of kilter and that he must take whatever steps are necessary to restore essential balance. To dream of murdering a parent does not say that the dreamer had an unhappy childhood. Rather, it suggests that the apron strings have not been totally severed as the dreamer would like them to be. Such a dream can persist after the death of both parents, indicating that the dreamer is still too tied emotionally to them. To see a murder warns that inevitable change is in the air and that if the dreamer can grin and bear it, the outcome will not be as bad as was feared.

Muscles

if they are as well developed as an athlete's, signify that enemies are about to show their faces but that you will see them off and come out of the experience with increased wealth. If the muscles are underdeveloped, then if you think you see success beckoning, don't be excited: it's calling someone else.

Mushrooms

denote unhealthy desires from sexual to financial matters. Anything acquired on either of these fronts may be lost through profligacy. Dreaming of eating them has, since the late 1800s, suggested, to quote one dream interpreter, 'humiliation and disgraceful love', and to paraphrase the words of another, death to those who dream of eating this fungus.

Music

can be good or bad. Heard being played tunefully it presages good times ahead. Heard being played badly it suggests that misbehaved children will cause disruptions in the house.

Musical instruments

generally herald that the outlook is good, unless they are broken, in which case, for men, anticipated pleasures will be marred by unexpected bad company. Strangely, for a woman to dream of broken instruments tells her that her future is in her own hands and that if she works hard enough there is little that cannot be achieved.

Nails

(the sort we hammer in to hold pieces of wood together, as opposed to our fingernails) are indicative of the dreamer's ability to hold things together. If they are obviously secure, then the dreamer is confident of this ability, but if they are loose, they may be indicative of a fear that life is about to fall apart. To some analysts, nails are associated with masculinity and sexuality. Again, if they are firm, the dreamer is secure in his sexuality, but if they are falling out, then there may be deep-rooted fears concerning this. Seers of days gone by believed that to see nails was to be told that you will work hard throughout your life for very little reward, but if the nails are bright and shiny that won't matter to you. Dull or bent nails were thought to herald a bout of illness or a phase when disorder of some sort would rule the day. And to hurt yourself while hammering in a nail was a warning to hold your tongue however tempting it may be to lash out.

Necks

if they belong to the dreamer, necks warn that there are family members, maybe of the extended family, who have a grievance about some business matter, perhaps a will, and that in the airing of it the dreamer's business affairs will be adversely affected. If it is someone else's neck that features then the dreamer should beware that someone very close sees him or her as being too worldly for his or her own good. And if a woman dreams that her neck is too swanlike, she should learn to control her temper or else she will become so increasingly shrewish that her children will bring forward plans to leave the nest. Worse, her husband may flee with them!

Negligées

as might be expected herald adventure in the love department, especially if the dreamer comes into contact with another who confesses to a similar dream! If the negligee is still in its box or bag, friendships being forged now will be long-lasting and the source of a great deal of pleasure. And for a man to dream of a woman clad in such a garment is a warning that he will be strongly tempted to stray from the marital bed, and that if he yields to it, the consequences will be almost unbelievably far-reaching.

Nephews

smiling through a pleasant dream say that good news, perhaps concerning a windfall, is about to be received. If, on the other hand, the man is frowning or is seen as being uglier than he is in real life, then there's some sort of disappointment ahead: nothing serious, but a disappointment just the same.

Nests

suggest that the dreamer treasures safety above all else and in so doing suspects that he or she has become over-reliant emotionally on family and close friends. Traditionally, to dream of an empty nest was thought to be a warning that business may be about to go through a difficult spell, while if there were eggs in it, then investments recently made will give good returns. And nestlings chirruping merrily were thought to denote safe and successful journeys.

Nettles

despite their obvious sting can prove beneficial if you dream that you are walking through them without being stung, for then prosperity beckons. If you are stung you are going to make someone, perhaps a partner, unhappy. Generally nettles are a warning to be stringent with your means. Nettle dreams go back a long way as they were the source of both food and drink in the Middle Ages. They are currently coming back into fashion, so there may be more nettle dreams.

Newspapers

are believed to be an indication that the dreamer is the sort of person who likes to have all the facts before coming to a decision, no matter how trivial. Some interpreters even go so far as to say that different types of newspapers have different meanings. For example, dreaming of a daily broadsheet suggests that the dreamer believes that the devil is in the detail in all aspects of life, while to dream of the weightier Sundays suggests that the dreamer is the kind of person who can assimilate information without appearing to do so. In the days when newspapers did not enjoy the wide circulation that they do today, it was thought that to dream of them was to be warned that any dishonesty perpetrated in the past would soon be uncovered.

Nieces

when seen in the dreams of a woman, warn that the immediate future will be peppered with worry caused by totally unexpected events.

Night

is the time when most of us relax, sleep and gather the strength needed to see us through the following day. To see it in dreams is to suggest that the dreamer is becoming aware that the time is drawing close when the decision to make a new beginning will have to be made, shaking off the old and embracing the new. Older generations of analysts believed that to have dreamt of the night was to be warned that oppression was about to blow in, to the detriment of the dreamer's business.

Nightgowns

tell the dreamer that career prospects are excellent, unless he sees the gown being taken off either by himself or another. In this case the dreamer is afraid that the consequences of some hasty and ill-considered action are about to bear fruit – and it will be too bitter to swallow! They can also warn that the dreamer may be about to be laid low for a few days with a cold or some other mild affliction. To see others in their nightgowns warns that there may be a downturn in business or career matters, and sad news about a friend not seen for a while may be about to be heard. If a lovestruck young man sees his girlfriend in her nightdress, then it's more than likely that another will take her place in his affections.

Nooses

with their obvious association with the hangman and the inevitable death that follows, are thought to suggest that the dreamer feels trapped, perhaps by his past but more likely by the actions and attitudes of other people. If this interpretation is accepted, then it is up to the dreamer to look to the past, come to terms with it and move on, or to shrug his shoulders at society and get on with life as he thinks it should be lived.

Nudity

often features in dreams. If dreamers see themselves in the nude, then scandal is in the wind and if the dream occurs just after appointments have been made, it may be best to consider cancelling them as they could have unexpected and unwelcome consequences. If the dreamer sees himself being suddenly discovered in the nude and desperately tries to conceal himself, then he is feeling guilty about something – usually some illicit pleasure that has been very much enjoyed. If other people are dreamed of in their naked state, then temptation will be put in your path. If a young woman sees herself admiring her naked form in a mirror, then she will win the respect and regard of an honest man – but not for long.

Numbness

can signify that a bout of mild ill health may be about to lay the dreamer low. It may be little more than a vague feeling of being under the weather.

Nuns

tell dreamers of religious bent that spiritual matters may be about to be pushed aside in favour of more material matters. If the dreamer is female, the good sister brings a warning of early widowhood or long-term separation from the man she loves.

Nurses

seen in the house suggest that the dreamer is concerned about their own health or that of someone close. If the nurse is a resident rather than a visitor, then an eagerly anticipated visit from friends will not go according to plan. In fact, if the friendship survives you'll be lucky. If, on the other hand, the nurse is being waved off, then good health is presaged. To see oneself in nurse's uniform, tending the sick, says that the dreamer will rise in the esteem of friends and employers. If the dreamer leaves the patient to attend to other matters then an acquaintance could be about to do their damnedest to persuade the dreamer to do something deceitful or that goes against the grain.

Nuts

gathering nuts has good auguries, not unconnected with amorous adventures. These usually involve new partnerships, which does not do much if you are currently in a happy relationship. Fortunately these same signs can be interpreted as an aid to prosperity in financial matters.

Oak

some of the oldest recorded dreams involve oak trees, inevitably connected to England. They are associated with security, emotional and financial. A tree full of acorns is the greatest symbol of increase, profusion and possibly an inheritance. But beware blasted oaks and falling leaves, which suggest exactly the opposite. Fanciful dreams of lovers under oaks suggest early marriage.

Oats

these do not feature greatly in dreams today but they were a mainstay of the diet when dreams were first recorded and could decide whether or not an agrarian community and its livestock could make it through a difficult winter. In general they are a good sign, suggesting a good harvest in the fields and at the hearth.

Obelisks

indicate that we are aware that we were born with a fundamental nature and that it is up to us to shape it to our best advantage. The more basic the obelisk is, then the more we are aware that there is still a great deal to do. But if it is ornately carved, then the better are we using our creative talents and the more instinctively do we lead our lives. An obelisk seen as being tall and totally unadorned indicates that we are presenting a very cold face to society and the dream warns us to change our ways unless we want to face a cold, lonely future. Obelisks are also phallic symbols and if the dreamer suspects that it has some sort of sexual connotation then its meaning can only be interpreted in the context of the entire dream.

Obituaries

may not make as sad a reading in the pages of a book about dreams as they can do in the pages of a newspaper, but they are unwelcome nonetheless. To dream of one presages that duties of an unpleasant nature will fall on the dreamer, while to dream of reading one says that news of an unsettling nature will awaken the dreamer from his daytime reveries.

Obstacles

can be either physical barriers that prevent us getting from place to place or emotions that stop us moving on from one situation to another and coping with each one as it appears. To dream of such an obstacle is to be aware that it exists and it is up to the dreamer to find the best way round it. Often, once the subconscious awareness has become a conscious realization, the battle to get over it is more than half-won.

Offices

often suggest that we feel burdened by responsibility and that we would like to relinquish if not all responsibility then at least share it. They also feature in dreams at times when work has become less enjoyable than it once was and at such times tell the dreamer to search for ways to make it more pleasant.

Ointments

soothe our cuts and grazes in real life and they bring good news in our dream world, too, for they say that new friendships are about to be formed and that they will be long-lasting and very advantageous to both parties. If the dreamer is a woman and she sees herself making an ointment, she is being given advance notice that she will soon be in a position to be in complete command of her own destiny in career matters and in affairs of the heart.

Olives

these do not loom large in northern culture, but should you dream of collecting them (usually with a band of jolly friends) business is going to prosper. Eating them, or even using their precious oil, tells of conviviality. Accidentally smashing a bottle of oil indicates possible small disappointments.

Omelettes

when being eaten warn that somebody regarded as an equal by the dreamer is about to impose upon him, probably financially. And flattery and deceit are likely to be experienced by the dreamer if he sees himself being served one.

Onions

being sliced and bringing tears to the eyes suggest that you will soon feel the sting of defeat at the hands of a rival. But otherwise, dreams in which onions feature herald good things. They tell of success (although the more there are, then the more will be the amount of spite and envy your success will generate). Dreaming of eating them presages that you will see off all opposition in your way to the top. If the onions are seen growing, then you will learn from the rivalry you experience.

Oranges

seeing them, good. Eating them, bad. Some of the earliest dreams have been associated with them as they have been confused with the 'golden fruit' of which Eve partook (actually an apricot) and the golden apples from the Garden of the Hesperides. If you dream of a fine one so high on the tree that you cannot reach it, it means you will one day make a fine and lasting relationship. As recently as the 1800s, when death loomed much larger than today, eating an orange and spilling its luscious juice suggested an impending death in the family. Perhaps A. A. Milne was right when he wrote 'the only safe place to eat an orange is in the bath'.

Orangutan

bellow unfaithfulness of some sort. Perhaps an acquaintance is using you to further his own ends at whatever cost to your friendship. For a young woman, to dream of this primate portends an unfaithful lover.

Orchards

strolling idyllically through an orchard with a partner is one of the greatest romantic images. But beware the fallen fruit – remember what happened in the Garden of Eden. It is unlikely to happen to you, but one of the earliest dream interpreters warned 'if you see a hog eating fallen fruit you will lose all your property, particularly if you have not been honest in acquiring it'. If the orchard is full of trees heavy with fruit, that tells that the dreamer can expect a life of abundance. However, if the trees are fruitless, then plans being laid will come to nothing and wealth that has already been accrued by the dreamer may start to erode.

Orchestras

presage a happy love life and good times on the horizon if the dreamer is one of the players. If he hears the music of an unseen orchestra, then he will be the centre of a happy circle of good friends.

Organs

being played at their thundering best tell the dreamer that friendships now being forged will be long-lasting and that plans concerning future financial security will flourish. But to see an organ in a church or chapel is a warning that someone in the immediate family is about to leave for pastures new, or worse, may die. If it is the organist rather than the instrument itself that is being dreamed about, the dreamer is being warned that the thoughtless actions of a friend will result in the dreamer's nose being put out of joint. If a woman sees herself sitting at an organ it portends that her lover will abandon her unless she succeeds in becoming less demanding, both emotionally and sexually.

Ornaments

can indicate that we feel undervalued in a relationship but that we have it in our power to do something about it. And we should do so very quickly if, like so many ornaments, that relationship is not to be put on a shelf and left there to gather dust. Dreams of ornaments can also suggest that the dreamer is of a financially extravagant nature and he is being given a warning to pull in his horns.

Orphans

are an expression of the dreamer's feeling of being unwanted and unloved and experiencing the resulting vulnerability. To dream of being orphaned is to be told that it is time for us to shake off the invisible apron strings, stand on our own two feet and accept that we can't live in the protection of others all our lives. A dream of being in the company of orphans used to be thought of as a sign that the dreamer's personal enjoyment was about to be sacrificed because of the unhappiness of others.

Osteopaths

are indicative of our need to manipulate the circumstances of our lives to ensure material comfort. They can also suggest that the dreamer is concerned about his health. To dream of an osteopath could say that an awareness is gradually growing in the dreamer's subconscious that he or she is being manipulated by another person or influences, either of which can be countered if that's what the dreamer wants.

Overalls

and suspicion for some reason walk hand in hand across the dream landscape! For an unmarried woman to dream that her boyfriend is wearing overalls serves as a warning that he is not all he has cracked himself up to be. And for a married woman to see her husband overall-clad is to be given advance notice that next time he claims to be away on a business trip, the business may not be the one in which he works!

Oxen

symbolize sacrifice, strength and patience. In dreams they can indicate a desire to be cast in a subservient role. Two oxen indicate that good times are just around the corner, especially if they are yoked to the plough. Scraggy beasts, though, indicate lean times in the offing.

Pain

if it is the dreamer's, pain suggests that some trivial action will lead to regrets that are out of all proportion. If it is someone else's pain, the dreamer is being warned that too many stumbles are being made in the march along life's path. If the discomfort is more of an ache, the dreamer is not being bold enough in business. He or she may have some good ideas but by not promoting them strongly enough, others are profiting.

Palm trees

these provide an ideal image for aspiration and escape. Walking down an avenue of such is the road to new beginnings and not just a blissful holiday experience (though perhaps these are the same two things). Recently a French writer suggested that they are heightened symbols of aspirations, but at almost the same time a British writer suggested that they symbolize the great height from which you could be let down by a friend.

Panthers

distress a dreamer and denote bad influences working against him or her that may result in contracts being cancelled or at least delayed. But if the panther is successfully slain, success is about to smile and banish any clouds looming on the horizon. If a panther's roar causes panic in the dreamer, bad news, especially about expected profits or bonuses, is in the offing.

Parachutes

are protective in dreams, suggesting that whatever life throws at us in our waking lives, we have sufficient emotional reserves to take it and get through to the other side safely. They can also indicate that the dreamer is seeking freedom from an emotional tie and the subconscious, by making the parachute appear in a dream, is telling the dreamer that this is the right course to follow.

Paradise

is closely linked to the fact that we all have it in us to be perfect – or at least we had until life tainted us with experience. To dream 'in Arcadia ego' is an expression that we are striving to achieve a balance between the perfection we desire and the knowledge that none of us can be perfect. On another level, to dream of paradise is an indication that the dreamer runs his or her life well and values honesty above all else. It also suggests that he or she has the ability to be successful and happy in whatever field chosen, as long as the principles by which life is lived at present are adhered to.

Paralysis

has meanings for businessmen and for lovers. For the former to dream of being paralysed is a sign that a downturn in the business cycle may affect them more than their rivals. To those in love, the same dream indicates that things will not go smoothly – indeed, the romance might well be heading for the rocks right now.

Parsley

being eaten portends good health. You may well need it for it could mean that you and your spouse have a large family. To see it growing suggests that success will come but that it will be hard won.

Peaches

so luscious when you are awake, peaches presage illness when in dreams, particularly where children are involved. Observing them growing prolifically is a better sign. You will prosper in your desired profession. Dried peaches, not exactly common, are a warning that colleagues may be conspiring against you.

Pearls

suggest that the dreamer's social life is in for a boost and that those in trade are in for a spell of good business. A young, engaged woman who dreams that she is wearing a string of pearls is being told that she has been lucky in her choice of lover. But if she dreams that the string breaks and the pearls cascade to the floor, then bereavement is presaged – perhaps not someone particularly close, but linked closely enough to cause some distress. And if a young woman sees herself looking at another's pearls with envy in her eyes, then her ambition to marry well and acquire wealth will be such that others will find it off-putting. Romany folk believe that a dream of pearls is a dream of tears, especially for brides.

Pears

may be golden on the bough, but are not so in dreams. Eating them reduces chances of success and even means health problems. Just seeing them suggests that your aspirations can prove a mirage. Harvesting them seems so profitable at the time, but will be followed quickly by disappointment. Perhaps this mirrors reality. Pears rot quicker than most fruit. At least dreaming of preserving them suggests that you can take setbacks philosophically.

Peas

at one time featured largely in dreams, no doubt because of their importance as a crop. Medieval peasants were not aware of Bird's Eye, which has probably reduced their importance to our psyche. Curiously, when canning was first invented, opening one can either revealed a lot of little problems or gave you momentary hope. Dreaming of dried peas suggests you are overstraining and as a result are likely to decrease life's pleasures and wealth.

Pens

serve as an indication that we need to communicate more with other people. If the pen is faulty and cannot be made to work, then it's likely that we have been given some information but have either failed to understand it or feel that we have not been given enough to take the appropriate course of action. The latter is reinforced if we dream that we lay the pen down to find another one but are unable to do so. Romany folk believed that to dream of a pen was to be warned that a love of adventure would lead the dreamer into some serious complications. And a pen that refused to write served as a warning that the dreamer was in danger of being charged with a serious breach of society's moral code.

Perfume

when received as a gift in a dream heralds good news if it is a scent that the dreamer likes. If it is not to his or her taste the news will be as disagreeable as the perfume. Good news is also predicted if the dreamer sees himself or herself giving someone a bottle of scent and it obviously pleases the recipient.

Perspiration

suggests that the road ahead is blocked with some sort of difficulty that will see you as the centre of unpleasant gossip. But don't get into a sweat about this. The difficulty will be overcome, the gossip will turn to words of praise and you will emerge from the experience with your honour not only intact, but indeed enhanced.

Pewter

is a metal that was once widely used but fell out of favour. Even so, it is still significant to the dreamer because it warns that circumstances may start to become straitened in the not too distant future.

Photographs

with their associations with times gone by, photographs indicate that the dreamer is looking to the past to help find a solution to a current problem. If dreamers dream they are looking

114

at themselves in a group photograph, they may well be in the process of rethinking relationships or attitudes. When photographs were a novelty, they were sometimes regarded with suspicion. This accounts for earlier interpretations, which include deception creeping up on the dreamer, false loyalties, suspicions regarding a partner's fidelity and being the unwitting cause of trouble.

Pianos

presage great joy ahead when they are seen but not heard. When dreamers hear lovely music being played on a piano they can look forward to a healthy, wealthy future. But if the music is tuneless and inharmonious then lots of little irritations are on their way. If the music is sad and wistful, then if sad news is not already on its way to you, it soon will be. To see a broken piano says that others may well hold the dreamer in regard but that he is not satisfied with what he has achieved. It also says that the dreamer's children will not do as well as had been hoped.

Picnics

are usually enjoyable affairs and this enjoyment is mirrored in their meaning to the dreamer — success and a cloudless sky are just ahead. If the dreamer is young, then hugely enjoyable times lie in store. But, if the elements interfere and the picnic is abandoned, then there may be hiccups in both love and business affairs.

Pills

being taken by dreamers foretell that more responsibility will be offered to them, but they will find the offer hard to swallow as they will soon realize that responsibility comes at a price. To be seen administering pills to others is a warning that others seem to be seeing you in a disagreeable light.

Pimples

can represent blemishes in our character, which we know will have to be dealt with – some time! They can also represent that although we are aware that we are being negative, we don't seem to be able to do much about changing our attitude to a more positive one. On another level, pimples tell the dreamer that he or she is far too concerned with trifling matters and that it's time to try to get the broader picture into perspective. To see others with pimply skin suggests that something another does or says will put brakes on the dreamer's rise up the ladder of career success, for a while at least. If the dreamer is a woman and she sees herself as being so pimply that people shun her, then she may have to mend her ways if she is to escape the wagging tongues of others in her immediate social circle.

Pirates

are indicative of the fact that there is something in the personality of the dreamer that is subjugating the emotional side. To dream of them is often seen as a sign that the dreamer feels that he or she is losing control of some aspect of life or, for a woman, that she feels that her partner has too much say in the way she behaves. To dream that you are a pirate is to be warned that you will fall from grace for some reason and former friends and family will come to look down upon you. If a young woman dreams that her lover is a buccaneer it portends that he is unworthy of her love and will deceive her cruelly in the future. If she is taken prisoner by a pirate, the silver-tongued words of someone will persuade her to leave home and if she does she will soon realize that she has made the wrong decision. For a male dreamer to be taken prisoner by a pirate suggests that he feels under threat of losing control of some aspect of his life.

Plays

are the thing, and the thing they mean in dreams depends upon the type of play and the sex of the dreamer. If a woman dreams that she is watching a play she is being told that she will receive many proposals from attractive suitors and that her choice will eventually be made for financial rather than romantic reasons. If she is on her way to the theatre and there is a hold-up of some sort, then unpleasant surprises are about to occur. These are also presaged by a play that is particularly bloody. If the play is a drama, then old friends who have been away for some time are about to reappear and the friendship will grow and become deeper than it used to be. If the drama is tedious and the dreamer is bored, then he may be about to be forced into the company of an unpleasant person. If the play is a comedy, then the immediate future is going to be filled with happiness. To be in the audience while a tragedy is being acted out foretells that great disappointments are about to cloud the sky and that a misunderstanding will make the sky even darker. And don't even ask what is about to befall you if you dream that you are in the cast rather than the audience, for 'troublous times' loom.

Polar bears

suggest that those who appear to be warm friends are in fact cold-hearted deceivers.

Poplar

once sacred to the Greek god Heracles, a poplar tree foretells that hopes will be fulfilled and that dreams of good things will come true – but only if the tree is green and is bursting with life. A withered poplar is a sad sight, and sad too will be the person who dreams of it, for disappointment will soon darken the skies.

Poppies

blooming and bobbing their red petals in a cornfield are one of the delights of the countryside. Sadly they signify no delights for the dreamer, for they warn that ill health will soon afflict the dreamer or someone in the immediate family circle.

Potatoes

unless they are dreamed of rotting, promise plenty. To dream of planting them portends that long-held desires are about to be realized. To see oneself digging them up promises that success will soon be harvested. If the potatoes are being eaten, a significant gain of some sort is about to be made. And to cook them suggests that career matters are bubbling along nicely and will get even better. The downside to potatoes sprouting in dreams is that if they are mouldy or rotting, then the pleasure in life will soon be a thing of the past and a dark future lies ahead.

Priests

are unwelcome visitors in the dream landscape, for they bring bad tidings with them. If the priest is in the pulpit, the dreamer may be about to be struck down with illness. For a woman to dream that she is in love with a priest suggests that her lover will deceive her: and if – Heaven forbid – she dreams that she is making love to a priest her love of laughter will not be smiled upon by those closest to her. To see oneself in the confessional box suggests that some sort of humiliation or sorrow is looming.

Primroses

may belong to a different family from poppies, but like them they carry a message that illness may soon strike and that whoever is afflicted will need to take great care.

Pumpkins

should be welcomed in dreams, especially by those suffering from a lonely heart, for they tell that the dreamers will soon be surrounded by admirers and that one of them could well turn out to be 'the one'.

Punch

for some reason, punch is often reported to feature in the dreams of those who have a reputation for being self-centred and who enjoy their pleasure at other people's expense. So if you dream that you are enjoying the punch bowl, perhaps it is a warning that it is time to mend your ways.

Pyjamas

with their connotations of bed and relaxation, pyjamas indicate that the dreamer would like to be more open about certain aspects of his life – his sexuality perhaps – but is unsure how to go about it.

Pyramids

suggest that change is in the offing – not one or two changes, but a whole barrowload of them. To see yourself climbing a pyramid means you have quite a journey ahead of you before you get what you want out of life. If it is a woman who has this dream, then she is warned that the man she plans to marry is not the one for her.

Quarries

suggest that the dreamer is digging deep into his or her personality, hoping to find something lurking there that will help solve a current problem. To dream of tumbling into one presages some sort of difficulty about to be faced either by the dreamer or someone close to him or her.

Queens

signify that the dreamer will be successful in anything he or she cares to turn his or hand to, unless the monarch is old and haggard in which case pleasures will recede to be replaced by serious disappointment.

Quicksand

denotes insecurity and lack of control over events that are seen as moving ahead at a gallop. The dream serves to warn the dreamer that he or she must move quickly if the dream is not to be translated into reality. To see oneself trapped by and sinking into quicksand suggests that the dreamer feels ensnared by a difficult situation of someone else's making.

Racquets

tennis, badminton or squash, denote that just as the dreamer thinks he has something he has long wished for within his grasp it will be snatched away from him. For a young woman to have this dream is indicative of the fact that something will happen to prevent her taking part in an event she has been eagerly looking forward to.

Radios

are a clear sign that communication is dominating the subconscious mind and suggest that the dreamer wants to seek the advice of someone he or she respects to talk through a problem in the hope of finding a solution to it. They also suggest a feeling that the advice that has been offered so far is not enough. When radios were a pleasant and, to many, an unaffordable diversion, they were said to signify that pleasure and prosperity lay ahead when they appeared in dreams, and that a new friendship would be made that would enhance the dreamer's prospects.

Radishes

presage that the kindness of friends will bring about business success. Eating them, however, suggests that one of these friends will act thoughtlessly and that in doing so there will be a little hiccup on the road to that success.

Railway tracks

suggest that the dreamer would do well to keep close track of business affairs as someone he trusts is plotting against him. If the dreamer is a woman, a visit to some friends who she has not seen for some time is heralded.

Rain

has several meanings. Torrential rain points to feelings of depression. Heavy rain suggests that the dreamer wants to be cleansed of something that has stained his past. Light rain suggests that the dreamer's life is about to change in some way. To dream of a deluge means that financial ruin is about to stare the dreamer in the face.

Raincoats

are a symbol of the need for protection from an onslaught upon the dreamer's emotions. They can also indicate that the dreamer has the desire to return to the womb, in the short term at any rate.

Red

is the colour associated with strength and physical energy. It can mean that renewed vigour is about to flow through the dreamer's veins, making him ready to face any challenge that life may throw in his face! It can also be taken as a warning that rage and anger, if allowed to go uncontrolled, will have an adverse effect.

Reflections

reflect our self-image, which may be stating the obvious, but that's what they do. They can warn that the dreamer is too concerned with how he is perceived by society. If he would only look beyond the superficial and try to explore what is behind what he sees, then he would come to enjoy a greater understanding not just of himself but of society in general.

Resignation

indicates that we have given up on something and we are not sure if in doing so we have made a huge gaffe or done the right thing. To see oneself as being resigned to something or resigning from a job says that the dreamer has tried everything to get through a particular situation and is no longer willing to invest the time and energy necessary to do any more. But other factors in the dream may indicate that there is still something that can be done if the dreamer is willing to explore just one last alleyway. Only he or she can decide whether or not to try it.

Resuscitation

has two meanings, depending on who is being resuscitated and who is doing the resuscitation. If it is the dreamer who is at the receiving end, significant financial losses could be about to make themselves felt, but the effect will be temporary. If the dreamer is resuscitating another, for new friendships are about to be forged and not only will they be enjoyable, they will enhance the dreamer's reputation – and maybe boost earnings.

Rheumatism

warns that plans being laid will be plagued with unexpected delays, if it is the dreamer who is affected. If it is someone else in the dream who is stricken, then disappointments will crop up when least expected.

Rhinoceros

if a rhino roars into your dreams, its presence foretells that a loss of some kind is looming on the horizon. The trouble it foretells is often of a secret nature – something you do not want the world to know about. If, however, you dream that you kill a rhino you will leap courageously over any hurdles in your lane.

Rhubarb

with its great leaves suggests a jungle and the glorious red stems are equally evocative. It grew in almost every garden not many years ago, but today is more likely to be harvested from supermarket shelves. Generally it is an omen of good, but to dream of cooking it suggests argument and a break with a friend. Eating it has also been thought to suggest great unhappiness with your present work situation.

Ribs

that are obviously healthy signify wealth, but if they are in poor condition then poverty will loom large in the dreamer's life. If the upper ribs are broken, and the dreamer is a man, then he is about to have some sort of disagreement with his wife and she will emerge victorious. If the lower ribs are broken, then the argument will be with female relatives rather than the wife, and once again the distaff side will win! If dreamers of either sex see their ribs growing larger and stronger it means a happy marriage is on the cards.

Rice

is traditionally scattered at weddings to bring the happy couple good luck, and also showers the dreamer with good tidings. It predicts success in business and that friendships made will be warm and long-lasting. Farmers who dream of rice can expect a bumper crop, and anyone who dreams of eating it is promised domestic harmony. A young woman who sees herself cooking rice can look forward to new duties coming her way, which will make her happier both in matters of the heart and the pocket! The only drawback to dreams of rice is if it is mixed with grains of soil, for featuring so in dreams warns that ill health is just round the corner and friends may move away.

Riding bicycles

is a good omen for men, not so good for women. For a man, pedalling uphill tells him that his prospects are getting brighter the harder he pedals. For a woman, however, to see herself riding downhill warns her that her good name may be about to be called into question and her health might be on the wane.

Riding motorcycles

tells the rider that he is firmly in the driving seat as far as personal relationships are concerned. To see someone else astride a bike is a warning that while all around you are doing well, you are at a standstill in your career and lovelife.

Rocking

is a comfort activity and as such suggests that the dreamer is trying to get in touch with real matters – to cast off the unnecessary trappings of life and rebuild the basics. In doing so, the foundations can be built on to create a more rewarding and consequently much happier life.

Rooms

are often regarded as dream symbols of various parts of our personalities or levels of comprehension. Each room has its own significance for the dreamer, but in general they are often taken as symbolizing the womb and the mother figure. According to lore, if they are richly furnished, they herald an upturn in fortunes. It might be in the form of a legacy or it might be that a gamble pays off in spades. For a young woman to dream of such a room is a sign that someone who at the moment is simply an acquaintance may be about to feature more significantly – very significantly in her romantic life and will eventually keep her in some considerable style. If the room is plainly furnished, then romance will bloom, but the suitor, while ardent, will be comfortably off rather than wealthy.

Rope

on one level suggests that the dreamer is ready to accept the responsibility that life is about to ask him or her to carry. It is often the case that these responsibilities have already been half-accepted, but that something has held the dreamer back from one hundred per cent commitment. The dream tells him or her that now is the hour. If the dreamer is tied to the rope, then perhaps there is a feeling of being constrained, especially at work. But if the dreamer takes the opportunity to stand back and decide what is really important, there is nothing to stop him or her cutting through the rope and moving on.

Rosemary

was, according to Shakespeare, 'for remembrance' but in dreams it has connotations of sadness. Although it adds delightful fragrance and taste to many real-life dishes, in dreams it bodes ill for relationships which, on the surface, may seem very happy.

Roses

are probably one of the more obvious symbols of everyday life. Dream of them blooming beautifully and your life will follow suit – you may even succeed in a love quest you previously thought hopeless. Smelling heavy fragrance of rose suggests a future of complete pleasure. On the dark side, withered roses show a lack of relationships and white roses (perhaps because of their drained look compared with the red varieties) suggest impending illness.

Roundabouts

of the type commonly seen at a fair curiously signify that the dreamer is about to experience a period where nothing will go right and that business affairs may start to stagnate. If the dreamer is a spectator rather than one of the carousers, then hopes will go unfulfilled and dreams will turn to dust. If the roundabout is standing alone with nothing else on the landscape, then a period of great unhappiness is about to descend on the dreamer.

Rowing boats

can be difficult to control and if someone dreams that the boat he is rowing overturns, he should beware of being asked to participate in a new business: more than likely it will go belly-up like the boat. But if the boat gets to its destination safely, the dreamer is all set to enjoy the company of sophisticated and amusing people.

Rum

presages a wealthy future but an increasing taste for gross behaviour that will cost dreamers the friendship of those who knew them while they were poor, or at least before they became wealthy.

Sailors

tell the dreamer to prepare to receive news from abroad. In days of yore, to dream of a sailor was to be warned that a dangerous sea voyage was imminent. On a deeper level, sailors represent freedom of spirit and freedom of movement and their appearance suggests that the dreamer is in control of his life more than most. That said, dreamers who see sailors in their dreams might need to seek the approval of someone in authority before making the most of that control.

Salad

may, in real life, be an essential part of a healthy diet but in dreams there are few omens other than bad ones. Eating it suggests illness, quarrels and meeting disagreeable people. Inexplicable, but that is the way of dreams.

Salt

signals disharmony. Plans will start to unravel and arguments will blow up from nowhere, especially at home. To see yourself salting meat implies that you may have taken out a larger mortgage than your income merits and that while you can afford the repayments at present, things may change for the worse. If a young woman sees herself eating salt, she will lose her love to a more beautiful rival.

Sardines

suggest that unexpected and distressing events are about to muddy the waters, and if the dreamer is a young woman and she is laying them on the table, then she is about to attract the amorous attentions of someone who is distasteful to her.

Sausages

being eaten indicate that while the dreamer's home will be a humble one, it will be one of warmth and happiness, which will act as a magnet to others. If the dreamer is making sausages, then he will be successful at whatever he may care to turn his hand to.

Scratching

the head tells you that fawning strangers are annoying you with their unctuous flattering, which, you are well aware, is self-seeking ingratiation of the most blatant kind.

Seduction

according to traditional dream analysts, seduction has two or three meanings, depending on the sex of the dreamer. If the dreamer was a young woman and she dreamed that she was being seduced, that was a warning to her to beware of being over-influenced by attractive extroverts. For the male dreamer, on the other hand, to dream that he was seducing an attractive young woman was a warning that he may be about to stand falsely accused of some misdeed. If the woman being seduced gives in, then she may well be attracted to what he offers on the worldly goods front rather than the loving one.

Sex

according to Freud is the very stuff of which dreams are made. Many dream symbols could somehow or other be put down to matters sexual no matter how distant or tortuous the connection seems to be. Fair enough, for when a child is born it is almost immediately aware at an obviously unexpressed level that it is no longer part of its mother's body: it has a life of its own and almost immediately the search for warmth, comfort and love begins. At first the mother fulfils these needs, but it is not long before the baby becomes aware that its sexual organs can provide them. At first this is via unintentional contact with them. Later it finds expression in the typical toddler's fascination with his or her own body and later through contact with others. Given this, and society's still sometimes prudish attitude towards sex, it is little wonder that deep-rooted guilt associations are formed and that as the child progresses to adulthood, this guilt is expressed in countless dreams! Briefly, dreams of sex allow the mature human to explore aspects of sex that were suppressed at childhood and to enjoy them. It is only when we awaken that guilt re-establishes itself! So sex in dreams is the subconscious's way of balancing this guilt with the natural need for sexual self-expression. Pre-nineteenth-century dream interpreters took a simpler view. To them, to dream of having good, pleasurable sex was a sign that personal relationships, not just sexual ones, were a source of great joy to the dreamer and that there was no reason to worry that they may ever be anything else. To dream of watching others having sex, on the other hand, suggested that the dreamer was unable to find fulfilment in his or her relationships – sexual or social. And to dream of having sex and finding it a burden rather than a pleasure signified that the dreamer was thinking about getting involved in a business undertaking but was concerned that if he did, the consequences may be unfortunate to say the least.

Shakespeare

with around 37 plays to his pen and quotes from many of them known to millions of us, Shakespeare has his own entry in the dramatis personae of dreams. To see the bard warns that unhappy times are in the offing, especially for those in love. For a young person to dream that he is reading Shakespeare is an indication that he has a deep love of literature and may well seek his career in publishing or a related occupation.

Shellfish and molluscs

have various meanings but often feature together in the rockpool of the dreamer's mind. Clams advise that thriftiness will pay off, even if some plans have to be temporarily shelved. Crabs have been cast in the role of bearer of news that a lawsuit may be looming, which if lost, could be financially ruinous.

Ships

are welcome in the logbook of dreams for generally they indicate that the dreamer will rise far above the station to which he was born. Ships sailing through stormy waters warn that business is about to take a downturn, probably because of the deliberate actions of a colleague or employee. And if the dreamer hears word of a shipwreck, then the perfidious person will in all likelihood be a woman! To lose one's life in a shipwreck warns that the dreamer will sail close to the wind and might be about to have a near-death experience. And to see others perish in a shipwreck indicates that a friend will turn to you to save him from the disgrace of bankruptcy.

Shirts

can be good or bad. If they are torn it could be that someone is spreading slander about the dreamer. If the rent is self-inflicted then it is the dreamer himself who has been indiscreet about someone and is worried that the consequences will be dire. But if the shirt is in pristine condition, success in a new venture is certain. To dream of putting on a shirt suggests the dreamer will enjoy a trouble-free spell for the time being and that travel to a foreign country is on the cards. There is a proviso to the last meaning: if the dreamer has recently embarked on a new affair, it's not going to last long, for he will soon be tempted to lay his head on another's pillow. Shirts can also mean that no matter what life throws at you, you will smile through your difficulties. To dream of losing a shirt is a sign that business is going to go through a bad patch or that love affairs are heading for trouble.

Shoes

tell us that we have our feet on the ground and that we have our finger on the pulse. But if the shoes are curiously designed then the dreamer may be being warned that he needs to take a fresh look at his attitude to life in general and that if this is done, the benefit will be felt in many departments of the dreamer's life. There is an old superstition that it is unlucky to put shoes, especially new shoes, on a table. This has spilled over into the dream world where such shoes are thought to be symbolic of death, physical maybe or perhaps in the form of a farewell to an old acquaintance. To dream of wearing new shoes is to be told that travel is in the air. And, curiously, to dream that one is shoeless suggests a comfortable and honourable life. If the dreamer sees shoes falling from his or her feet it indicates poverty and distress. And if the shoes are scruffy and down at heel, then you will be short of cash more often than not.

Shooting game

is a pointer to the fact that the dreamer may be motivated by selfishness but he will probably get what he aims for. If the game comes within range but manages to evade capture or death, then the dreamer had better start paying more attention to business matters or else a considerable loss may be experienced.

Shoulders

dreamed of as naked say that the dreamer will shrug off any bad luck and that changes of a pleasant nature will make him view the world in a much nicer way.

Shrouds

serve as a warning to the dreamers that they should take better care of themselves as their health may be about to be called into question. They can also say that a false friend will cause the dreamer some sort of financial hardship and will enjoy seeing the deep distress this causes. If the dream concerns a shroud being removed from a corpse this is a warning that a squabble, if not patched up quickly, could deepen into a bitter argument that will never be completely healed.

Silk dresses

have two quite contradictory meanings according to two dream experts from days gone by. According to one, for a woman to see herself dressed in silk is a sign that, if unmarried, she will soon meet her lover who will be rich, and if she is already wed, her husband will become wealthy. But the other interpretation suggests that for a married woman to see herself dressed in silk is a sign that her husband is being unfaithful with a woman who will cause him financial distress.

Singing

says that good news is wafting or is about to waft its way towards the dreamer, unless the song is a doleful one, in which case then things might be about to take a turn for the worse. If it's a bass voice, then the dreamer would do well to keep an eye on business matters, for an employee could be taking advantage of a laissez-faire attitude. For those in love, a deep singing voice warns that tiffs and quarrels could be about to become more common. A duet says that bad news about an absent friend is about to be received, but that will bring a little light relief. Choir music presages that the cobwebs of gloom are about to be blown away, unless the dreamer is a woman, in which case her lover might be about to be tempted by the attractions of not just one but several other women.

Skeletons

when seen in dreams warn of oncoming illness or, worse, injury inflicted by someone who has misunderstood something you did or said and is out for revenge. If the dreamer sees himself as a skeleton, then he is worrying unnecessarily about something and should lighten up. If a skeleton is seen as haunting the dreamer, then there is trouble ahead – perhaps an accident or financial disaster.

Skulls

signify that there are domestic squalls about to blow in, which, while they will die out, will leave an atmosphere of suspicion that will linger for some time. If it is the skull of someone known to the dreamer, then a friend is about to turn enemy because the dreamer has in some way been preferred. If it is the dreamer's own skull that is seen, then he or she is about to rue something said or done.

Smoke

signifies that doubts and fears will puzzle you. Try to ignore them because there really is nothing to worry about, unless you dream that you are overcome with smoke. In that case, a silver-tongued flatterer is about to victimize you.

Sneezes

signify a change of plans is on the cards, if the sneeze is your own. If it is someone else's sneeze then you are about to have unexpected visitors who will bore you to distraction.

Snow

is said to mean that prosperity is about to enrich the dreamer's life. If he is already prosperous, then he will become even more so. That is the interpretation put upon snow by Romany folk: other dream interpreters say that to dream of snow is a warning that while there will be no real misfortunes in the dreamer's path through life, there might be bouts of ill health that could affect career prospects. To dream of eating snow is indicative that ideals will never be realized. If the snow is grey and dirty it warns that pride goes before a fall and that the fall is just around the corner. Such snow can also mean that someone you have been holding in contempt will do something to redeem themselves in your opinion and that you will take the necessary steps to bring about reconciliation. A dream that you are looking through a window at a fall of large white snowflakes warns that financial depression will cause rows with your sweetheart. If you dream that you are snowbound, wave after wave of bad luck is about to crash down upon you. And a final word on the meaning of snow in dreams – to see the sun shining on a snow-covered landscape says that the dreamer may be facing financial difficulties at present but that the sun will shine on his endeavours to overcome them and that he will prosper.

Soldiers

are interpreted as a warning that conflict of some sort may be about to march into the dreamer's life. The background to the dream may give some clue as to how the conflict will arise and how it will eventually be settled. The arrival of the military in a dream can also say that deep down the dreamer has realized that there is a need for him or her to be more self-disciplined. And it can also mean that a change of employment is just around the corner.

Sons

if he is dreamed of as being unusually good looking, a son can be regarded as a sign that the boy will be particularly successful at anything he puts his mind to and will bring great honour to the family. But if he is in any way blemished or seen to be suffering from illness or the results of an accident then there is trouble in store.

Sores

portend that illness will cause you considerable financial loss and may affect your mental balance for a short time. If the dream concerns dressing a sore, then your own dreams and desires will have to be given second place to the pleasures of a third party.

Spring

when dreamed of as suddenly appearing out of nowhere in a dream, forewarns that something is not right in the dreamer's life and that whatever it is will soon crawl out of the woodwork and play an increasingly large and unsettling part in things. If the dreamer sees the buds of spring starting to bloom and the season progresses sweetly into summer, then all's well and the dreamer can look forward to prosperous times in business and the company of good friends.

Sprinting

in a race suggests that others share your ambitions and that whoever puts his mind to it will be first to break the winning tape. And it could be you!

Squeezing

into dream clothes that are obviously too tight suggests that the dreamer has outgrown things that were once a source of pleasure and is looking around for new amusements.

Stairs

and staircases often feature in the dreams of those who are aware that there are certain steps that have to be taken before goals are achieved. Climbing the stairs suggests that the goal may be a spiritual one. Going down a set of stairs, curiously, suggests that the dreamer is concerned that his or her sexual techniques might not be keeping his or her partner happy! To dream of falling down stairs is a sign that others are seeing you with envy, or worse, hatred in their eyes. Seeing others descend a staircase warns dreamers to enjoy the good times while they can, for there are a few squalls on the horizon.

Stings

warn that your current happiness is about to be pierced by an unexpected event.

Stockings or tights

warn to be alert for trouble or distress of some sort, for it is not far away. And if they are laddered or have holes in them then best mend your ways if you don't want to be the subject of wagging tongues. If the stockings are white, a mild bout of illness may be ahead. Stockings can also mean that the dreamer is about to look for his or her pleasure in places associated with the dissolute.

Straw

if seen burning in dreams, once a common sight in the countryside, straw suggests prosperity, but straightforward bales of straw suggest an empty life. If the dream concerns feeding animals on straw, this suggests that the dreamer has not made sufficient provision for his or her nearest and dearest.

Stretchers

carry their own message – and it's not a particularly pleasant one. To see yourself stretcher-borne means that you will soon be asked to undertake some task or accept a job that is distasteful, but that you will have no option but to grin and bear it! And to see a stretcher is a harbinger of bad news – not tragic or deeply upsetting, just mildly disagreeable.

Sugar

may be sweet, but it sours our dreams, suggesting as it does that in the foreseeable future the dreamer will find fault where there is none, particularly in domestic matters. And that this will be emotionally and financially draining. Eating sugar indicates that unpleasant matters will have to be dealt with, but that the outcome may be better than at first expected.

Surgeons

suggest that the dreamer is acknowledging that there is something in his life that is unwanted and should, if possible, be cut out as soon as possible. Seen wielding the scalpel, they suggest that the dreamer has business enemies who are plotting to get their own way at the dreamer's expense. For a woman to see herself on the surgeon's table is a warning that a bout of ill health is about to hit her.

Surgical instruments

say that a friend may be about to cause concern by appearing to withdraw the hand of companionship and to be remote for no reason that the dreamer can think of.

Swellings

dreamed of are a good sign in that they say that the dreamer will build a substantial fortune by working hard. However, self-importance will inflate the dreamer's ego and stop him or her enjoying his or her good fortune.

Swimming

has a variety of meanings because, in the language of dreams, water is symbolic of our emotional life. If we see ourselves swimming against the current, we are probably aware that we are acting in a fashion that is against our own nature.

Swimming in crystal-clear water is an indication that we have done something of which we are deeply ashamed and that we have a deep-seated desire to be cleansed of it. If the water is dark, then depression might be about to cloud our lives.

Sycamore

for a single person to dream of this proud tree signifies that marriage is on the horizon, or if not marriage then a lifelong commitment to another. But if the dreamer is already married, the sycamore suggests that the green-eyed monster of jealousy will soon turn his gaze in the dreamer's direction.

Syringes

warn that bad news about a relative's health is on the way. But relax, for it will prove to be a false alarm and whoever has been sick will be well on the road to recovery even before the bad news is received. If the syringe is broken, then what might appear to be trifling little mistakes at work will cause a ripple effect that will have totally unexpected ramifications.

Taffeta dresses

tell the women who dream they are wearing them that they will be wealthy, but that money doesn't buy happiness!

Tambourines

are not usually heard in dreams so it is appropriate that their meaning indicates that an enjoyable event will happen in an unusual location.

Tattoos

needling themselves into your dreams are an unwelcome sign that something is about to happen that will necessitate a long and extremely boring absence from home. If the tattoos are decorating another's body, then someone is jealous of you and their jealousy is eating away at them, which may lead them to take unpleasant action.

Taxes

suggest that the dreamer is aware that everything in life has to be paid for in some way or other. If there is no difficulty in raising the money to pay the dream tax and if the dreamer is happy to pay it, then this can be taken as a sign that the dreamer is reasonably content with life – even if the pleasures he most enjoys are of the forbidden variety. To be seen struggling to pay or to begrudge the money is a sign of guilt. A refusal to pay tax indicates that the dreamer takes an unconventional view of life and lives it according to his own rules rather than those respected by the rest of us.

Taxis

have two meanings. If the journey is during daylight hours, then the dreamer's career prospects are no better and no worse than anyone else's. If it's dark outside, then you will be party to a secret that must be kept from everyone – at any cost.

Tea

has a variety of meanings. Dreamed of being brewed, it signifies that the dreamer will find himself charged with the crime of indiscretion, and rightly so. Forgiveness will be a long time coming. Drinking tea with friends, although it may seem contrary, suggests that the dreamer would rather put his free time to better use than socializing with others. To go to a tea caddy and find it empty warns that gossip of a disagreeable nature is being whispered about you. Lastly, someone who dreams that he is 'dying for a cup of tea' is about to have his peace shattered by unexpected and unwelcome guests.

Teachers

are the first authority figures that most children meet outside the immediate family, and they may say that the dreamer is acknowledging the need for guidance to help overcome a problem which, while not pressing at the moment, could easily become so. They can also suggest that the dreamer has already been given some advice on how to cope with a pressing problem but that he is willing to consider an alternative – indeed would welcome one.

Teasing

indicates an awareness that society is frowning on the way the dreamer conducts himself or herself, if he or she is the one being teased. Curiously, if the dreamer is the teaser rather than the teased, this is thought to be the subconscious's way of highlighting the dreamer's own idiosyncrasies. To dream of teasing can also be a sign of insecurity and a slowly dawning awareness of the dreamer's doubts and fears about some aspect of his or her personality. Such doubts and fears probably result from a childhood experience that was long forgotten. Remember, the memory forgets nothing. In centuries gone by, teasing was thought to denote a cheerful, well-mannered personality that would make the dreamer much sought after in society and successful in business. But for a young woman to dream that she was being teased was a sign that she would give her heart too quickly and that she would live to regret it.

Teeth

have almost as many meanings as there are teeth in the human jaw! To see ordinary teeth in a dream suggests that illness is about to strike or that new acquaintances may turn out to be wolves in sheep's clothing. Loose teeth warn that bad news about a business failure is probably already winging its way towards you. If a tooth is being extracted, then a serious bout of ill health is waiting in the wings: the only good news is that it will not turn out to be fatal, although it may be touch and go! Dreams of losing one's teeth warn that pride goes before a fall, especially in business matters. To have a tooth knocked out means bad luck will come out of the blue. It could be a business failure or it could be the death of a loved one. This litany of bad luck gets worse if the teeth are yellow and crooked, for such teeth herald loss of property, a bout of bad health (probably affecting the nervous system) and being let down by a business partner. If one tooth falls out, then look for bad news in the morning's mail. If two come loose and fall out circumstances over which the dreamer has no control will cause unhappiness. For three to fall out, a serious accident is presaged. And if the dreamer sees himself as having a full set one minute and being toothless the next, then hunger is about to gnaw at the dreamer's innards. The only time teeth smile on the dreamer is when dreamers see themselves gazing in a mirror admiring their mouthful of white, even teeth, for then their plans for future success will be brought to happy fruition.

Televisions

when being viewed by the dreamer, a television indicates that you are too easily swayed. This message is reinforced if what you are watching is making you feel uncomfortable. To see your own face on television is a sign that your friends see you as vain and shallow as a puddle, and this may lead to your heart being broken.

Theatres

are often seen during the sleeping hours. To dream of being in the audience foretells new friendships are about to be forged and that they will bring much happiness into the dreamer's life.

141

But while, for members of the audience, things should run smoothly in the immediate future, a dreamer who sees himself in the cast should make the most of the good things in life for they may be about to evaporate. If the show is a variety one, then the pursuit of pleasure may start to cost the dreamer dear in business affairs. If a pantomime is in progress, then assumed friends might soon reveal themselves to be false. An opera on the other hand says that friends are about to add significantly to the quality of life and that things will go smoothly in career and business matters. Someone who sees himself applauding or laughing in the theatre may be about to turn his back on duty and embrace fanciful pursuits. If for some reason the theatre has to be evacuated, the dreamer should think twice before getting involved with a business proposition.

Thermometers

warn that disharmony might be about to make itself felt at home and spill over into the office as well. If the thermometer is not working, then a bout of annoying rather than serious ill health could be about to afflict the dreamer. If the mercury is on the way down, the work front could be about to present a few problems, but if it is rising, then you are about to shrug off bad luck and experience a spell of good fortune.

The underground

signifies a bumpy ride ahead, probably on the emotional front. And if the train grinds to a halt between stations then the dreamer will soon find himself on the horns of a moral dilemma.

Thieves

who steal into your dreams during the hours of night are linked with a fear of losing something – maybe something tangible or perhaps something emotional instead, but a loss nonetheless. They can also suggest that the dreamer is increasingly aware that precious time is being squandered on a useless activity.

Thirst

warns the dreamer that what is being aspired to at present may prove unattainable unless the thirst is eventually quenched.

Thistles

alert the dreamer to the fact that he may be perceived as being defiant and vindictive by colleagues and acquaintances and that unless he puts his house in order this view could start to have some serious ramifications. Single thistles can indicate that the road ahead is plagued with minor difficulties, while to dream of a field of thistles suggests that the dreamer should follow another path altogether.

Thunder

predicts business reversals, while to be caught outdoors in a thunder storm warns that grief is about to wrap its arms around the dreamer!

Ties

are seen as representative of a desire for correctness and discipline in the dreamer's own life and business and in those of his friends and colleagues.

Tigers

may be a threatened species but if you see one prowling towards you, you will be threatened by torment and persecution by your enemies. And if it pounces, you will fail in some venture and be shrouded in gloom. But if you see off the attack, success will bless all your undertakings.

Toadstools

appear overnight in fields and gardens. When they appear in dreams they signify that the dreamer is due sudden elevation in career matters.

Tomatoes

were once thought of as toxic and dangerous to eat. That belief has long since fallen off the vine and today, to dream that one is eating tomatoes is a sign that happiness is about to appear, but like the fruit itself which rots after a few days, the happiness will be short-lived.

Tongues

if they belong to the dreamer, are unwelcome in the dream land-scape for they tell that for some reason friends will frown on the dreamer and that unless the dreamer mends his or her ways, then friendships may well start to evaporate. If it is the tongue or tongues of others that feature in dreams, then the dreamer is being warned that he or she may well find himself or herself at the centre of some scandal. To dream of a swollen tongue or one that is otherwise in poor condition tells the dreamer to watch his or her tongue. If the warning goes unheeded, careless talk could well cost lives.

Topaz

says those who dream of it will enjoy deep friendships and good companionship throughout their lives. But for a woman to dream that she loses something made of topaz warns her to be on the lookout lest recently made friends prove to have wormed their way into the dreamer's circle for their dubious purposes. To be given something made of topaz, on the other hand, suggests that she is about to embark on a brief love affair that will go unnoticed and that will end amicably on both sides.

Tornadoes

say that disappointment is about to blow into your life, especially if you have been banking on some long-laid plans coming to successful fruition. They won't! Tornadoes can also be seen as a suggestion that the dreamer feels threatened by a surge of emotions that could blow him off course. This interpretation can be taken as a suggestion that he is aware that if he makes some changes then he will be able to keep his feet on the ground and weather the storm.

Toys

tell the dreamer that the family will be a source of ever-increasing joy, as long as the toys are in reasonable condition. If they are broken, some sort of heartbreak is foretold. To see children playing with toys says that happiness will smile on the dreamer's marriage. To see oneself giving away toys suggests that friends and acquaintances will give one the cold shoulder. Toys are also thought to highlight the creative part of the dreamer's life and they may point to the fact that the dreamer is open to new ideas and new ways in which he or she can relate to other people. And it may be that when toys feature in a dream, the dreamer is being told that he or she is working too hard and to take some time off to relax and have some fun.

Trains

that are progressing smoothly along a railless track suggest that worries over a business opportunity recently grasped will prove unfounded and that money will soon start to flow in. But to see a freight train says that your career is on track and that you could be in for an unexpected promotion. If you see yourself settling down for the night in a sleeper then beware, for you are fast acquiring the reputation for being someone who is unscrupulous in the pursuit of wealth. If a dream train is travelling at breakneck speed, foreign travel is forecast, perhaps related to a promotion at work. If it breaks down, don't depend on business affairs going well: they probably won't. A train heard approaching says news from abroad is whistling down the line towards you, again probably to do with work.

Treacle

on the dream table signifies that a pleasant invitation is about to wing its way to you and that in accepting it you will find that surprises of an extremely pleasant nature lie in store. But if the treacle is eaten, you will be crossed in affairs of the heart. If a woman dreams that treacle is trickling on to her clothes, she will be surprised by an offer of marriage from someone she holds in contempt.

Trees

represent so many aspects of our lives that it is hardly surprising that they have a wide variety of meanings and to mention them all would result in a book with many more pages than this. To be brief, a tree with new foliage appearing means your greatest hopes are on the verge of consummation. Climbing trees is an obvious symbol for aspiring to better things. Cutting one down or pulling it up by the roots shows a wasting of your energies. Falling leaves are symbolic of what we have or hope to cast off, while the fruits of the tree represent what we have created in life. A tree seen growing mirrors a subconscious desire for growth, in the physical, emotional or psychological area. A dead tree may foretell that the grim reaper is about to wield his scythe, or that something we value will pass from our lives. To dream of branches laden with fruit and bright with green leaves is a portent of wealth and the opportunity to spend time with friends. But if the branches are barren, there is likely to be bad news of long-lost friends. Withered leaves tell that hopes will rise only to be dashed almost immediately, and if the dreamer is a young woman marital happiness may evade her forever. Blossom-covered trees promise prosperity, while to see roots spreading warns of decline in health and business.

Trumpets

when seen but not heard foretell that something unusual but extremely interesting is about to happen. If the dreamer is blowing his trumpet then his good fairy is about to wave her wand and make his dreams come true.

Trunks

foretell that Lady Luck has turned her back on the dreamer, unless he or she is packing the trunk, in which case an enjoyable journey is on the horizon. If what was in the trunk is now scattered in disarray around a room, a journey will have to be planned at extremely short notice, maybe as the result of a quarrel, and the outcome will be far from satisfactory. An empty trunk warns that the search for romantic attachment will end in disappointment.

Turnips

being eaten signify ill health is about to strike. If they are being pulled up by the roots, on the other hand, there is a general improvement in store as new opportunities will soon present themselves and a corresponding upturn in fortune will result. If they are seen growing in the field, then again, prospects are about to brighten.

Turquoise

when it makes its occasional appearance in dreams, tells the dreamer that in achieving an ambition of some sort, he or she will bask in the approval of family and friends.

Umbrellas

the word comes from two Spanish words that mean 'shade the lady' and they shelter us from the elements, sun as well as rain. When seen in dreams they indicate that we enjoy the shelter offered to us by a friend or a colleague. They can also be seen as a sign to the dreamer that improving skills and further education could be the keys to providing shelter later in life. To dream of carrying a rolled-up umbrella in the rain suggests that business plans are about to go awry, while a leaky one denotes quarrels with loved ones.

Uncles

may be good fun in real life, but when they make an appearance in a dream they warn that news of some sort that will cause a family dispute is on the way.

Underclothes

cover our most intimate parts and so it is not surprising that they are thought, when dreamed of, to be concerned with our most intimate secrets.

Undressing

puts us in touch with our sexual being and indicates a need to reveal our true feelings about someone or perhaps about a situation concerning which we have not been true to ourselves. If we are watching another person getting undressed, it may be a sign that while we are aware that we should be more sensitive to other people's feelings we don't do much about it. So the dream serves as a wake-up call to become less self-centred emotionally than we are. To dream that we are taking another's clothes off indicates a need to understand something about ourselves, which is slowly stirring in the very depths of our being. Dream analysts of times past believed that to dream that you were undressing denoted a rift with a loved one because of the scandalous behaviour of one or other of you. To see someone else undressing presaged bad luck in love and money, while to dream of being undressed by someone else was thought to be a sign that flirtation would lead to romantic disaster.

Unemployment

is not a particularly happy state when awake and is just as negative in dreams. It suggests the dreamer is feeling undervalued and is scared that he or she will not be equal to a task that has to be faced in the immediate future.

Uniforms

suggest that the dreamer has influential colleagues and friends keen to help him climb the ladder of success. If uniforms feature in the dreams of a young woman then the man on whom she bestows her affections will return it – in spades. But if she sees herself slipping out of a uniform and changing into more relaxing attire, her love of adventure will lend a note of notoriety to her name to such an extent that she will find herself at the centre of a scandal of her own making! Dream characters wearing strange uniforms suggest that disruption is in the air – a friendship that has run its course and is brought to an end, perhaps.

Urgency

when it is the feeling that stands out most in a dream, urgency can be taken as a warning that you have overlooked something very small. But unlike the rolling stone, it will gather moss and become bigger and bigger and assume an importance out of all proportion to its original size. So if you have this dream sensation, go through the fine detail of your life, leaving no stone unturned. Other factors in the dream may give a clue as to where you should be looking. If you are being asked for urgent advice, then something may well be about to crop up that will require a little financial juggling on your part.

Vaccination

to the male dreamer, vaccination says that he is too susceptible to the charm of ambitious females who will unscrupulously use him for their own ends. For both sexes to dream that they are vaccinating others suggests that no matter where the dreamers look to find happiness and contentment, these will be constantly elusive. And for a young woman to see herself being vaccinated in the leg means she should keep her sense of smell alert for the whiff of treachery in the air.

Vaults

can suggest that the dreamer is aware that something of a sexual nature may be stirring and may soon come to play a significant part in his or her life. They can also represent our store of collective knowledge, something that increases as we age and which is always there when we need to draw on it. Indeed, to be seen going down into a vault suggests that we are already aware of this and are on the verge of exploring it to see how it can help us in several aspects of our life. To be seen burying something in a vault was seen by gypsies as a sign that dreamers would soon suffer a sad loss. And to dream of burying something valuable in a vault was a warning to be on the lookout lest someone try to cheat you out of money or land.

Vegetables

in general indicate that you have been deceived into believing yourself to be successful while all the time you have been badly used by another. If the vegetables are rotten great sadness is about to engulf you. If a young woman dreams that she is slicing vegetables then she will cut off her nose to spite her face and cause her lover to leave. But that turns out to be no bad thing, for a new love will soon show his face and prove to be a faithful husband.

Veils

either covering someone else's face or your own suggest that whoever is wearing them has hidden agendas and may resort to dishonesty before showing their true hand. If matters of the heart are on the dreamer's mind, then deep down he is well aware that he has not been totally sincere with his lovers and when this is revealed, underhand methods may have to be used to retain their affections. If a young woman sees herself losing her veil then her lover realizes that she may have been unfaithful. Bridal veils herald welcome change in the dreamer's life and for a young woman to dream that she is wearing one is a suggestion that a recent investment has been a wise one and will pay handsome dividends. But if the veil comes loose, there's sadness in the air.

Velvet

clothes appropriately signify that honour and riches could be there for the asking, if the dreamer recognizes the opportunities that come his or her way and grabs them.

Ventriloquists

have an obvious meaning to dreamers and that is to be warned to take nothing at face value. If someone gives you advice think carefully before acting on their words, especially in the case of business matters. For a dreamer to see himself as the voice behind the doll, then he is not acting properly towards people who trust him.

Vicars

and other non-Catholic men of the cloth can herald that a period of calm is on the horizon and that any disputes will soon be settled to the mutual satisfaction of everyone involved. They can also indicate that the dreamer acknowledges that there is still much for him or her to learn, especially regarding the spiritual side of life. Vicars can also portend that jealousy and envy will lead you to do some extremely foolish things. If the dreamer is female and dreams that she is marrying a man of the cloth it says that the man she loves does not return her affection and that she will either die a spinster or marry for the sake of it. Dour Presbyterian ministers in a dream may suggest that change of an unpleasant nature is in the air and that that may necessitate an equally unpleasant journey. If the minister is preaching, then dreamer beware for someone you know will try to tempt you off the path of righteousness! And to dream that you are a minister suggests that you have your eyes on someone else's property and will be quite unscrupulous in getting it.

Vinegar

is not to be welcomed. It predicts disharmony in every aspect of life. To dream of drinking it indicates that you will be forced to commit to something against your better judgement and that this will cause you tremendous worry. And to see yourself drizzling it over your food implies that something that is already causing you distress is going to get even worse.

Vines

are generally a sign of success, happiness and great health. Visiting a vineyard suggests an auspicious love-making partnership. But if anything is seen withering on the vine, beware. Business schemes in particular are likely to fail.

Violet

tells the dreamer to fuel the altruistic and spiritual side of things and that if this is done, then the benefits will spill into every aspect of his or her life.

Violins

say to the dreamer, 'Relax. You are the centre of a warm, loving family and our financial affairs are in perfect order.' If the violin is more fiddle than Stradivarius, that message is reinforced and as a bonus, a trip overseas will soon create a happy diversion from humdrum, everyday living. When a young woman dreams that she is making sweet music on a violin she can expect an honour of some sort, accompanied by rich gifts. But if her music is out of tune, then she will soon find herself falling out of favour with her friends and the things to which she aspires will never be hers.

Visits

in the sense that someone is seen calling on the dreamer, indicate that we are aware that what we need – be it comfort, information or love – is out there waiting if only we know where to look. That is if the dreamer knows the visitor. If it is a stranger who comes knocking at the door, then he or she may represent a facet of our personality that has long been unrecognized, but that is now trying to establish itself in the dreamer's consciousness. To be seen making a visit is significant of a need to widen the horizons if life is to be lived to the full. According to folklore, to dream of a visitor clad in black is to be warned of accidents waiting to happen. And if the visitor is obviously weary after a long journey, then although the actions of family or friends may cause displeasure, it would be better to keep your feelings to yourself, for if you give them voice they may cause wounds that will never be healed.

Waiters and waitresses

seen in dreams mean different things depending on whether the dreamer is doing the waiting or being waited on. If it's the former, then we are acknowledging an awareness of our ability to care for other people. If it's the latter, then it's the dreamer who is looking for that care.

Wakes

be they of a suitably solemn nature or the more raucous traditional Irish variety, tell the dreamer that he is subconsciously aware of a need to grieve over something that has gone from his life. It may not be a person: perhaps it is a phase of life, a friendship, whatever – but something gone for ever. And once the grieving is over, the dream says that it is time to move on, to grasp new opportunities, accept that ageing is an unavoidable part of life and make new friends. Wakes also suggest that the dreamer is acknowledging that the support of friends and colleagues is needed if a disappointment is to be overcome. Traditionally, dreams in which a wake played a central part told the dreamer that a long anticipated engagement would have to be cancelled to make room in the diary for a meeting of an unpleasant kind. And for an unmarried young woman to dream that she saw her young man at a wake suggested that despite her best intentions to keep herself chaste until she walked down the aisle, his silver-tongued smoothness would persuade her otherwise – something she would come to regret deeply.

Walking

is an indication that we want to move forward, to explore life and all that it offers. If we are walking purposefully then we know where we are going but if we are ambling aimlessly, then we are being told that it's time to create goals for ourselves. If we are enjoying a pleasant walk in the countryside, then deep down we wish to return to the state of innocence in which we were so happy as children. If we see ourselves as using a walking stick, then we are acknowledging our need for the support of others. A pleasant stroll through the countryside says that separation from good friends will be a cause of great unhappiness but that there may be compensation in that business affairs will bloom. But if the walk takes us through rough terrain then tangled business affairs will cause misunderstandings that will turn warm friends to indifferent acquaintances.

Walls

can be good and they can be bad. If the dreamer sees one block the way ahead, then losses are signified in business dealings probably brought about by listening to well-meaning but ill-informed advice. To see yourself jumping over a wall means that obstacles that present themselves will be cleared, while to break through one, you will achieve your ambitions but only after a long, hard slog. Knocking a wall down suggests that enemies had better look out, for you have the scent of victory in your nostrils and are not to be beaten. A young woman who dreams that she is walking along the top of a wall is being given advance notice that plans she is laying down to secure her future happiness are well founded. But if she dreams that she is hiding behind a wall, then she has probably formed an attachment with someone she would rather the world did not find out about.

Walnuts

are both good and bad in equal quantities. A fresh walnut when the shell is opened suggests great happiness and a favourable life. A decayed nut tells you that your great expectations will end in nothing.

155

Wardrobes

have two meanings, both of which depend on how full they are. Seen bursting with clothes a wardrobe suggests that in trying to appear better off than the dreamer really is, he is putting what money he already has at risk. If the wardrobe is almost empty, then flirtation is in the air: not of a romantic nature, but flirtation with danger. Beware!

Warts

say to the dreamer that he or she is looking at the world through distorted eyes. But there's no distorting the fact that dreams featuring warts say that someone is suggesting that your name and honour are not exactly synonymous and you may have quite a struggle to quell such talk. If you dream of having warts on your hands one minute and then seeing them vanish the next, then any obstacles you encounter on the path to good fortune will be easily cleared. And to see them afflicting others suggests that your enemies are gathering and plotting against you.

Whirlpools

suggest that the dreamer is about to be caught up in danger, especially if he is involved in running a business. It could be that the ripples caused by some sort of personal scandal will cause customers and colleagues to think again before finally committing themselves to a project that was almost signed and sealed.

Whisky

when seen but not tasted, whisky tells the dreamer that he or she can work as hard as possible to achieve an ambition, but it will never be realized. If the dreamer does down a dram then the dream will be achieved, but only after disappointments have had to be faced and overcome.

156

White

with its associations with purity and honesty, white predicts that innocent pleasures and freedom from pressures lie ahead. But it can also indicate that the dreamer is subconsciously aware that his life is colourless.

Widowhood

is not a happy state for most women and when a woman sees herself as one, she is being warned that malicious gossip will cause her much distress. If a man dreams that he is getting married to a widow, then his best-laid plans, probably business ones, are about to go totally awry.

Windows

warn that in some aspect of life that the dreamer holds dear, hope is about to be replaced by despair. And no matter how much effort is put in to restore things to what they were, it will take some time for that to happen, if indeed it ever does. If the windows are closed, then someone close to the dreamer may be about to jump ship! And if the glass is broken, then people you love might be about to accuse you of disloyalty.

Wine

promises that new acquaintances will become increasingly good friends. If a wine bottle is seen to smash in your dreams, then love may turn to passion and passion to excess. To dream of a wineglass suggests that serious disappointment is about to cloud your life.

Winter

when it blows into a dream, winter warns that a bout of ill health is on the cards and that things on the business front may become a bit frosty before a little sunshine sets in. Gypsies believed that in days immediately following a winter dream, no matter how hard the dreamer tried to achieve something, his efforts would yield absolutely nothing.

Wives

no matter how happy the marriage in real life, wives tell the dreamer that the immediate future may be a bit unsettled, unless they are unusually jolly, in which case recently made investments will pay off handsomely.

Wombs

suggest that the dreamer is seeking security and shelter. He feels he has been asked to shoulder an unfair share of responsibility and now is the time that the burden be removed.

Women

have several dream meanings, one of which is that intrigue could be being plotted behind the dreamer's back. If the dreamer is arguing with a woman then the plotters will be foiled. To see a dark-haired woman suggests that for some reason you will drop out of a race in which you were thought to have had a good chance of success. If she has auburn hair, a period of anxiety could soon hit the dreamer. And if she is a blonde, then the anxiety gives way to pleasure.

X

marks the spot in dreams as it is said to do in life. If that X is dreamed of as being on a treasure map, then according to gypsy tradition the goals you have set yourself are in sight and will earn you your just reward. A more modern interpretation is that to see an X is to be warned that something recently done in all innocence may turn out to be unwise, but that it is not too late to undo it before any damage results. If the sign is more of a cross than a recognizable letter of the alphabet, then it may indicate that a sacrifice of some sort has recently been or is about to be made.

X-ray machines

rarely feature in dreams. But on the odd occasion that they do, they serve as a warning that someone in a position of some power is delving into the dreamer's life trying to uncover a secret which, if unearthed and made public, could cause considerable distress to the dreamer. So if there is something in your past that you would prefer to stay there, make sure that your secret is safe, or remember the old adage that confession is good for the soul; it could also be good for your quality of life.

Yawning

in dreams can indicate the same as it does in life – boredom! What it is that the dreamer is bored with only he or she can say. It could be a job, a friendship, a love affair, whatever. Yawning can also suggest that the dreamer is forming an opinion about something but is not yet ready to give voice to it and will not do so until every option has been examined and thoroughly thought through. On another level, yawning can also be seen as a warning to control one's own abusive tendencies or to try to bring the abusive behaviour of another under control. To see someone else yawn is to be warned that a close friend may be about to fall seriously ill or get into financial trouble. Whichever it is, the dreamer will be called upon for help, which will be gladly given.

Yellow

the colour associated with cowardice, yellow suggests that the dreamer is afraid of facing a confrontation that he is aware is looming but will put off dealing with until it is literally staring him in the face. But the colour yellow suggests that if positive thinking is used and that the dreamer lets his head rule his heart then all will be well.

Yew trees

sacred to the Romans and used by British archers to fashion their bows, yew suggests that considerable wealth is about to line the dreamer's coffers. The wealth may walk hand in hand with honours of some sort being showered on the dreamer.

Yielding

in a dream is to be aware that a situation has reached a point where only direct confrontation with another person would seem to be the answer, but to know that such confrontation will be useless. In this circumstance it may be best to step aside and go along with the majority, even though you know they're wrong! On a spiritual level, yielding can suggest that the dreamer has been aware there is more to life than material success and that the time is right to do something about it.

Zebras

according to gypsy folklore, zebras indicate misplaced friendship and ingratitude. But other dream analysts hold that these fleet-footed creatures suggest that the dreamer will enjoy successful, if fleeting, enterprises.

Zips

are often seen in dreams as symbolic of our ability to develop relationships with other people. Put simply, open zips suggest an open nature, the ability to make friends easily and to keep the fires of friendship burning for ever. On the other hand, a closed zip indicates a tendency to hold back from offering the hand of friendship until you are absolutely sure.

dream
diary

dream diary

date:

content:

interpretation:

dream diary

date:

content:

interpretation:

dream diary

date:

content:

interpretation:

dream diary

date:

content:

interpretation:

dream diary

date:

content:

interpretation:

dream diary

date:

content:

interpretation:

dream diary

date:

content:

interpretation:

dream diary

date:

content:

interpretation:

dream diary

date:

content:

interpretation:

dream diary

date:

content:

interpretation:

dream diary

date:

content:

interpretation:

dream diary

date:

content:

interpretation:

dream diary

date:

content:

interpretation:

dream diary

date:

content:

interpretation:

dream diary

date:

content:

interpretation:

dream diary

date:

content:

interpretation:

dream diary

date:

content:

interpretation:

dream diary

date:

content:

interpretation:

dream diary

date:

content:

interpretation:

dream diary

date:

content:

interpretation:

dream diary

date:

content:

interpretation:

dream diary

date:

content:

interpretation:

dream diary

date:

content:

interpretation:

dream diary

date:

content:

interpretation:

dream diary

date:

content:

interpretation:

dream diary

date:

content:

interpretation:

dream diary

date:

content:

interpretation:

dream diary

date:

content:

interpretation:

dream diary

date:

content:

interpretation:

dream diary

date:

content:

interpretation:

dream diary

date:

content:

interpretation:

dream diary

date:

content:

interpretation:

dream diary

date:

content:

interpretation:

dream diary

date:

content:

interpretation:

dream diary

date:

content:

interpretation:

dream diary

date:

content:

interpretation:

dream diary

date:

content:

interpretation:

dream diary

date:

content:

interpretation:

dream diary

date:

content:

interpretation:

dream diary

date:

content:

interpretation:

dream diary

date:

content:

interpretation:

dream diary

date:

content:

interpretation:

dream diary

date:

content:

interpretation:

dream diary

date:

content:

interpretation:

dream diary

date:

content:

interpretation:

dream diary

date:

content:

interpretation:

dream diary

date:

content:

interpretation: